EXPLOI
EASTBO
AND THE
SOUTH DOWNS

David Harrison

S.B. Publications

To my wife Vivienne

First published in 1995 by S.B. Publications
c/o 19 Grove Road, Seaford, East Sussex BN25 1TP

ISBN 1 85770 0775

Typeset and printed by Island Press Ltd.
Tel: 01323 490222 UK

CONTENTS

Front Cover: Eastbourne from near Beachy Head

Back Cover: Beachy Head

Title Page: The Seven Sisters and Coastguard Cottages

Photographs by Tony Bannister

EXPLORING EASTBOURNE AND THE SOUTH DOWNS

Exploring anywhere immediately conjures up the mystique in most people. It goes back to when we were children when everything was new and everywhere needed to be explored. Even with the advancement of age nothing changes. To venture into "unknown territory" still stirs the imagination as it always did; to investigate round the next corner – to peep over the brow of the next hill . . . That is what this book is all about. To introduce the reader to the hidden nooks and crannies of an area of outstanding natural beauty in and around the coastal resort of Eastbourne.

The official definition of the word "explore" is 'To travel or range over with the view of making discovery, especially geographical discovery'. It is hoped, with the aid of this book, the visitor will make several discoveries. Eastbourne itself has much to offer, not only as a resort with its many attractions but with a history going back over a thousand years.

Then, with the aid of two separate short driving tours, the delights of some of the loveliest villages in Sussex – indeed England – will become apparent. Simply by following the easiest of directions the tours will guide the motorist from one attractive place to another pointing out places of interest en route, giving details on parking and providing information on each place in turn.

Even for visitors without their own transport this feast of exploration need not be missed for most of the places mentioned are accessible by public transport, details of which are also included in the pages that follow.

For those wishing to penetrate still deeper into this beautiful area no fewer than 8 walks are included again with simple step by step directions, instructions on points of access, full description of everything of interest on the way along with details of toilet and refreshment facilities where available.

All in all it is hoped that this account of Eastbourne and its surrounding area will help satisfy the curiosity and provide the impetus for many enjoyable outings in this delightful part of Sussex.

EASTBOURNE – A SHORT HISTORY

Early Neolithic farmers first settled in the area we now know as Eastbourne with very little changing over the centuries even during the Roman occupation.

Several villas were built during the first century AD although farming still continued as an important activity, the Romans merely exploiting existing communities.

With the coming of the Saxons many of the Roman ways were abandoned although there has never been much existence of Saxon habitation in the area. The earliest known reference was in an Anglo-Saxon charter of around AD963 when habitation was described to the east of the Bourne Stream, mentioning also a 'landing place' suggesting early maritime trading in the area.

Bourne, as the area was then known, was granted a church by Edward I in 1054 and so the Parish Church of St Mary was built and the thousand year history of the Eastbourne we know today had begun.

Following the Norman Conquest, William's half-brother Robert, Count of Mortain, held the manor of Bourne and by the time of the Domesday Survey it had become established with a church, watermill and several saltpans. The first phase of the present church was completed between 1160 and 1190 with further additions in the 14th century.

Around this time Bourne changed from its ancient arable farming traditions to pasture farming, partly due to the plague but more likely because more and more people began moving to the towns which were developing rapidly now.

By the 16th and 17th centuries Bourne's prosperity declined in common with the rest of the county. Hailsham, with its regular market, began to flourish but still the community at Bourne continued to centre round the parish church with little change until well into the 19th century.

The first Royal visit to the town was in 1780 when four of George III's children spent their summer holidays here but it was to be another 70 years before it was ever considered developing the town as a seaside resort. In between fell the troubled times of the Napoleonic War when a serious threat of invasion was apparent all along the south coast.

Following Royal Naval action in Corsica during the Revolutionary Wars whereby a tower manned by French troops at Mortella Point repulsed two warships with serious damage and many casualties, similar fortifications were considered ideal to protect the southern coastline and 73 were built between Folkestone and Beachy Head.

These were complimented by two large fortresses – called Redoubts – at Dymchurch and Eastbourne.

Today Eastbourne's seafront stretches primarily between the Redoubt and Martello Tower number 73 – familiarly known as the Wish Tower – so called because the Wish, a marsh fed by the sea, existed then in the near vicinity. Why the towers became known as Martello Towers is a mystery. Legend has it that over the years they became a corruption of Mortella Towers, after the Corsican affair, although another theory was because of the Navy's familiarity with watch towers on the Italian Adriatic coast called "torri di martello".

Modern Eastbourne owes its development to two local landowning families, the Gilberts and the Cavendishes. In 1792 the Manor House at Bourne was bought by Charles Gilbert and it was his grandson John Davies Gilbert who, with the help of the second and more powerful Cavendish family (who originated in a village of the same name in Suffolk and were well established at court in London from the 16th century) who saw to the development of the town.

Much of the Cavendish wealth had been acquired through marriage and astute speculation which was how they came to hold the estates of Eastbourne. The family were also the Dukes of Devonshire and it was William Cavendish, as 7th Duke of Devonshire, who largely was responsible with John Davies Gilbert for the elegant layout of the town.

By the 1870's the population of the new Eastbourne had risen to almost 7,000 and the Burlington, Grand, Queen's and Cavendish Hotels were all open now. In 1883 Eastbourne became a Borough and still the building continued until the death of the 7th Duke in 1891 when the impetus seemed to die with him.

In 1911 the town received County Borough status and by the onset of war three years later was considered among the largest and most exclusive holiday resorts in England.

During the twenty years between the wars Eastbourne continued to develop as a holiday resort. Parks and gardens were laid out, the bandstand was built and acres of adjoining Downs were purchased to prevent development. Then came the Second World War and drastic changes once France fell and the risk again of enemy invasion. The seafront was closed and the beaches defended with barbed wire. With the onslaught of flying bombs more high-explosive bombs dropped on Eastbourne than any other south coast town and the destruction was extensive.

Today, with a population of over 77,000, Eastbourne retains its elegance as the south's premier resort with the Cavendish family still forward looking to improve the town's facilities into the next century.

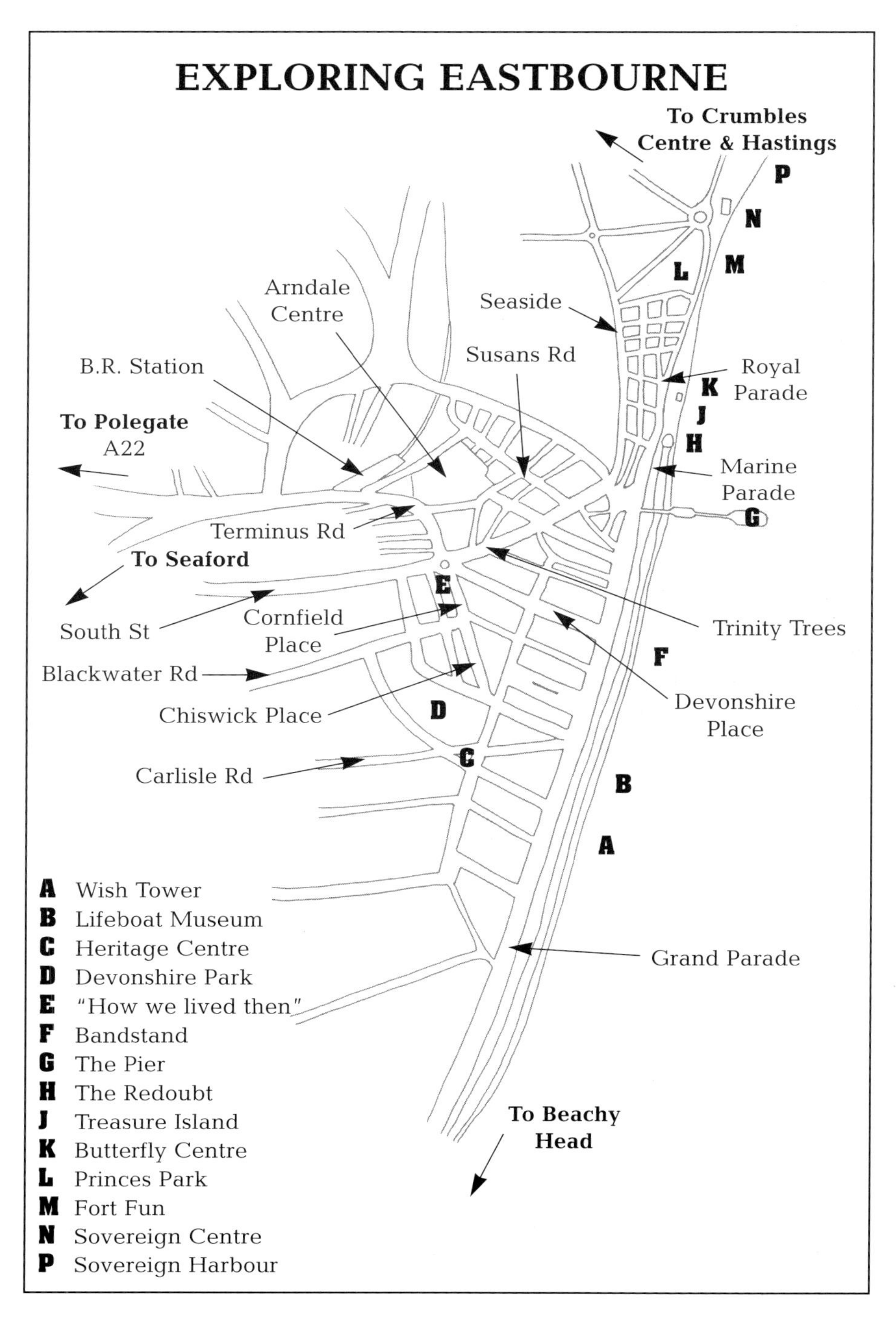
EXPLORING EASTBOURNE
To Crumbles Centre & Hastings
P
N
M
L
Arndale Centre
Seaside
Susans Rd
B.R. Station
Royal Parade
K
J
H
To Polegate A22
Marine Parade
G
Terminus Rd
To Seaford
E
South St
Cornfield Place
Trinity Trees
F
Blackwater Rd
Devonshire Place
Chiswick Place
D
C
Carlisle Rd
B
A
A Wish Tower
B Lifeboat Museum
C Heritage Centre
D Devonshire Park
E "How we lived then"
F Bandstand
G The Pier
H The Redoubt
J Treasure Island
K Butterfly Centre
L Princes Park
M Fort Fun
N Sovereign Centre
P Sovereign Harbour
Grand Parade
To Beachy Head

PLACES OF INTEREST

Eastbourne has the finest seafront of any other resort in the country. Nowhere can match its wide, three-tiered promenade noticeably lacking in bingo halls and amusement arcades. Nowhere can equal the magnificent 'carpet gardens', made up of more than 30,000 plants and flowers laid out over a century ago in the oriental design of Persian carpets, the display changed twice each year; or the elegant sweep of hotels and historic buildings that look majestically out to sea; or the strains of a military band playing in a regal bandstand or so many other little things that make this place so unique, so relaxing, so popular.

So many of the attractions of Eastbourne are centred on this splendid stretch of seafront without detracting from the elegance of its character. For easy location of each attraction on the town plan simply identify the letter prefix.

(A) THE WISH TOWER

Built in 1810 as part of the coastal defences against a Napoleonic invasion it contains over half a million bricks and took two years to complete. It was never used for its original purpose although during the Second World War it once again was called upon as part of our coastal defences, never firing a shot in anger. It was derequisitioned in 1947 and declared an Ancient Monument 12 years later.

The Wish Tower

(B) R.N.L.I. LIFEBOAT MUSEUM

Housed in an old boathouse adjacent to the Wish Tower, the museum was the very first Lifeboat Museum to be established in England. It features the history of Eastbourne's lifeboats from 1853 onwards along with various types of life saving equipment. A large range of souvenirs are available for sale.

Open Daily throughout the season (9.00 a.m. to dusk). Free admission. Tel: 01323-730717.

(C) HERITAGE CENTRE

Situated on the corner of Carlisle Road, the old Flag Tower and Manager's residence of the Devonshire Park and Bath's Company opposite the Winter Gardens was built in 1880 and houses a unique exhibition showing the grandeur of Victorian Eastbourne with the aid of many maps, photographs and models. Also included is an audio-visual show displaying the story of Eastbourne in comfort.

Open Daily (except Saturday) throughout the season (2.00-5.00 p.m.). Admission charge. Tel: 01323-411189.

(D) DEVONSHIRE PARK

In 1872 the Devonshire Club was founded for the benefit of visitors and residents and two years later Devonshire Park was opened for 'high class recreation'. Today its name is world famous for its sporting facilities, particularly tennis, for the pre-Wimbledon ladies' tennis championships are held here in June each year attracting all the top names in ladies' tennis.

Close by are the four principal theatres of the town, the Congress, Winter Gardens, Devonshire Park and Royal Hippodrome Theatres bringing between them a variety of top entertainment with well known stars and West End productions.

International Tennis Championships (booking enquiries): 01323-412000. Central Box Office (all theatres): 01323-412000.

(E) "HOW WE LIVED THEN" MUSEUM OF SHOPS

Just along from Devonshire Park, down Chiswick Place leading into Cornfield Place, is a late Regency townhouse built in 1850 which houses a century of shopping (1850-1950) with over 50,000 exhibits amassed over 35 years. Set out over three floors the displays include Victorian-style streets, wartime rationing products and old toys and games of yesteryear along with many more items of nostalgia and interest.

Open Daily 10.00 a.m.-5.30 p.m. (with possible Winter variation). Admission charge. Tel: 01323-737143.

(F) BANDSTAND

Situated on the Grand Parade, the Victorian bandstand hosts brass and silver band concerts which are held regularly during the summer season (last week of May to first week of September).

For times and details of concerts telephone or visit the Tourist Information Centre. Tel: 01323-411400.

The Bandstand.

(G) THE PIER

With the coming of the railways to Eastbourne in 1849 it was envisaged an increasing number of people would visit the town to indulge in the new Victorian craze of holidaying by the seaside. In consequence of this the Pier Company was set up in the early 1860's to erect a pier that was proving so fashionable with the Victorians. Bickering impeded the erection of the pier for almost ten years and so the increased prosperity the coming of the railways would bring to the town did not happen for another decade or so. Today the pier houses a variety of eating places and entertainments including amusement arcades.

Speedboat trips and water skiing are also available from the end of the Pier during the summer season, weather permitting. Tel: 01323-765559.

The pier is open all year (8.00-2.00 a.m.). Free admission (although several of the facilities are chargeable). Tel: 01323-410466.

The Pier.

(H) REDOUBT FORTRESS

A large, partially restored Napoleonic Fortress built between 1805-1810 to accommodate ten guns and a large garrison of soldiers. Today it is an ideal setting for a museum of the Sussex Combined Services and the

The Redoubt.

exhibits and displays cover most branches of the Sussex Military from Roman times to present day. A Centurion Tank 'guards' the entrance. Many special events are held including the famous 1812 Nights on Wednesdays and Fridays during the season.

Open Easter until early November (9.30 a.m.-5.30 p.m.). Admission charge. Tel: 01323-410300.

(J) TREASURE ISLAND

A children's adventure playground with paddling pools, Spanish Galleon, slides, climbing net, pedal go-karts and tricycles.

Open daily (10.00 a.m.-6.00 p.m.) during the summer season (April-September). Admission charge. Tel: 01323-411077.

(K) BUTTERFLY CENTRE

Enter another world: that of the tropics, recreated into a tropical garden with lush undergrowth including bougainvillaea and hibiscus, lake and waterfall and hundreds of live butterflies from all corners of the world. See all the stages of the butterfly's fascinating life cycle. Photography inside is permitted. There is also a gift and coffee shop.

Open daily (10.00 a.m.-5.00 p.m.) during the summer season (April-October) (last admission 4.30 p.m.). Admission charge. Tel: 01323-645522.

(L) PRINCES PARK

Situated at the eastern end of Royal Parade, Princes Park has beautiful flower displays, a boating lake and miniature golf course. The park has unrestricted access throughout the year although boating and golf are only available during the summer season at a nominal charge.

Tel: 01323-415465.

(M) FORT FUN AND ROCKY'S ADVENTURELAND

A two acre fun park designed specifically for the under 12's in which children can recreate the excitement of the Wild West with Western Train Ride, roller coaster, grass sledging, Astroglide, roundabouts and much more. Adjoining is a go-kart track and **Rocky's Adventureland,** the largest soft indoor adventure playground in Sussex. The ideal place for birthday parties.

Fort Fun is open during the summer season (Easter to end October) each day at 10.00 a.m.-6.00 p.m. (later in summer). Free entrance with 'Pay as you ride' system.

Rocky's Adventureland (indoor play area) is open every day of the year (except Christmas Day and Boxing Day) at 10.00 a.m. Admission charge.

Fort Fun.

(N) SOVEREIGN CENTRE

One of Europe's largest indoor water leisure centres, it comprises of four pools, a wave-making machine, two water flumes, jacuzzi pool, fitness suite and sports hall. A separate children's play area is fully supervised along with a bouncy castle and training pool. For the serious swimmer there is a 33-metre lane pool and separate diving pool. Inside is a shop, continental piazza with bars and cafeteria.

Open daily all year. Admission charge. Tel: 01323-412444 (information service) and 01323-738822 (office).

(P) SOVEREIGN HARBOUR

Situated at Langney Point and developed by the Tarmac Group, the £500 million marina is one of the largest in Europe. A 1930s passenger ferry *The Earl of Zetland* has been converted into a floating bar and restaurant, which is an ideal setting to sit and relax while watching the boats arriving and leaving the harbour centred around two basins, one tidal and one accessed through two locks (see page 11).

Sovereign Harbour – Tel: 01323-470099. Earl of Zetland Restaurant – Tel: 01323-470216.

OTHER ATTRACTIONS

Children's Seaside Fun. *Tel: 01323-415465.*
Punch and Judy (Wish Tower Slopes) and Sparky the Clown (Bandstand).
August to end of September. Admission charge for children.

Crazy Golf. *Tel: 01323-415465.*
Situated next to Treasure Island.
Open daily from 10.00 a.m. (April to end of October). Weekends and holidays only in October.

Dotto Trains. *Tel: 01323-641984.*
Land trains running from Holywell to Sovereign Harbour.
April to end of October. Daily from 10.00 a.m.

Eastbourne Golfing Park. *Tel: 01323-520400.*
'Pay as you play' 9-hole golf course situated at Lottbridge Drove.
Open all year from dawn until 10.00 p.m.

Formula Fun. *Tel: 01323-642833.*
Honda-powered Formula One Go-Karts.
Easter-mid October. Daily 10.00 a.m. to 6.00 p.m. (later in summer).

Miniature Steam Railway. *Tel: 01323-520229.*
Lakeside rides on a miniature steam train.
Open daily in the summer with additional opening times at Easter and weekends only in April, May, September and October.

Froggies Funland. *Tel: 01323-470220.*
Children's indoor adventure playground situated at The Crumbles Centre.
Open daily except over Christmas and New Year's Day.

Motcombe Swimming Pool. *Tel: 01323-410748.*
Situated at Motcombe Road, Old Town.
Open daily all year. Telephone for session times.

Brass Rubbing. *Tel: 01323-731366.*
All Saints Church, Susans Road.
Open Monday-Friday (2.00-4.30 p.m.) mid July to mid September.

Trax Indoor Karting Centre. *Tel: 01323-521133.*
46 Brampton Road, Hampden Park Industrial Centre. Indoor karting circuit. Minimum age 9 years. Refreshments available. No experience necessary.
Open all year – Daily (10.00 a.m.-9.00 p.m.).

TOWNER ART GALLERY AND LOCAL MUSEUM. *Tel: 01323-411688 (Information) and 01323-417961 (Office).*
High street, Old town.
For details, admission and opening times see page 30.

Finally, the most visited and most spectacular attraction of all is the natural scenery soaring up from the west of the seafront, the most famous sea cliffs in Britain – **Beachy Head.** A massive 575 feet high (175m) the cliffs totally dwarf the lighthouse below whose beam can be seen by ships 16 miles away (27km). This is the start of the South Downs, an 80 mile (133km) ridge visible from almost anywhere in Sussex; solid chalk, formed by millions of miniature sea-shells that lived and died beneath an ancient sea.

It is no accident that a 100-mile (166km) long distance footpath begins from the foot of the Downs, initially along 6½ miles (11km) of arguably the finest stretch of sea-cliffs in Britain then to stretch inland, never to touch the coast again. Details of seven walks along the South Downs Way are included in a separate section at the end of this book.

For details of further attractions and villages on the outskirts of Eastbourne there now follows two separate driving tours with full directions on where to go, where to park and what to see en route.

The Earl of Zetland Restaurant, Sovereign Harbour Marina. *(Photograph by Steve Benz)*

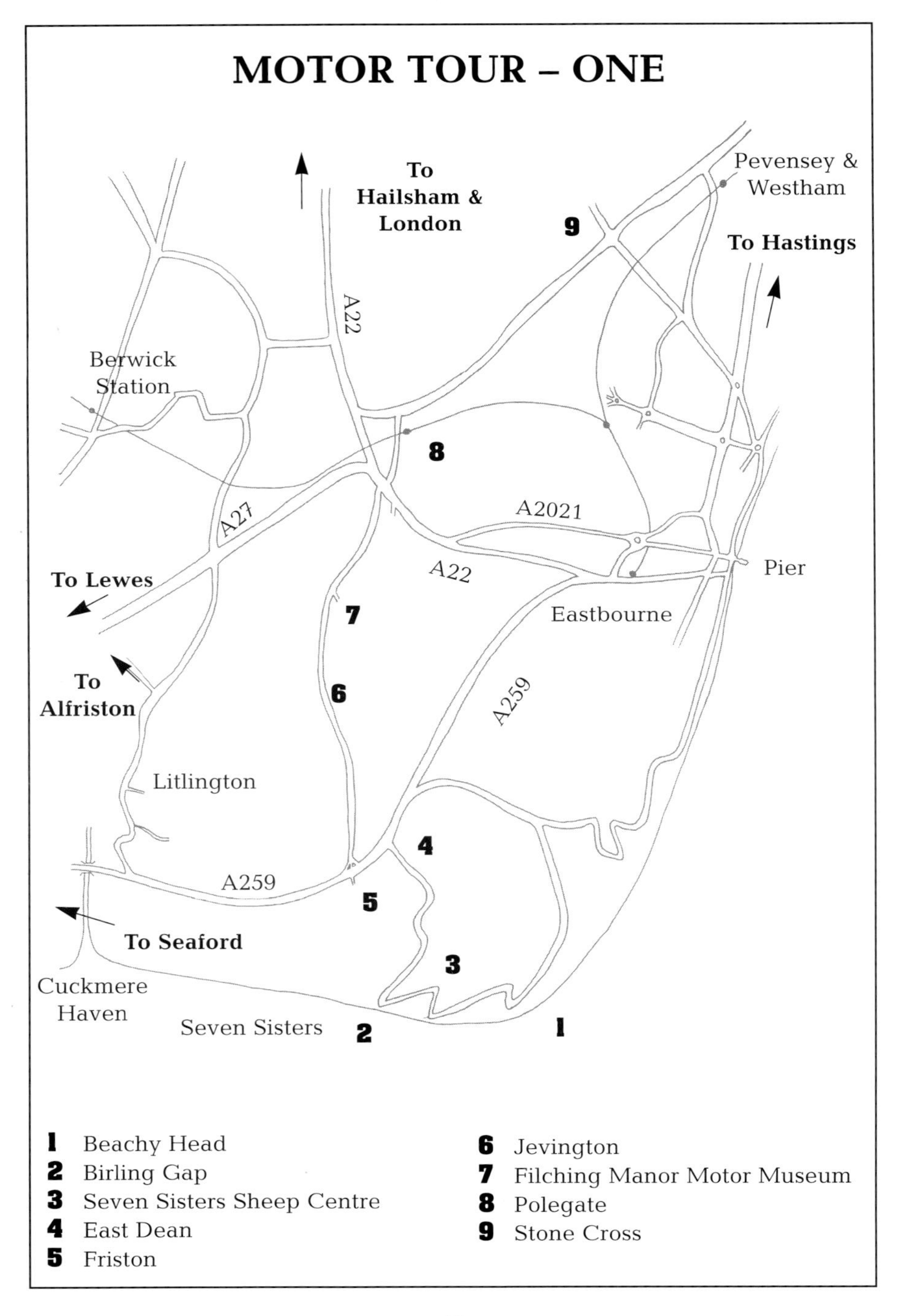
MOTOR TOUR – ONE
To
Hailsham &
London
9
Pevensey &
Westham
To Hastings
A22
Berwick
Station
8
A27
A2021
To Lewes
A22
Pier
7
Eastbourne
To
Alfriston
6
A259
Litlington
4
A259
5
To Seaford
3
Cuckmere
Haven
Seven Sisters
2
1
1 Beachy Head
2 Birling Gap
3 Seven Sisters Sheep Centre
4 East Dean
5 Friston
6 Jevington
7 Filching Manor Motor Museum
8 Polegate
9 Stone Cross

MOTOR TOUR – ONE (21 miles/34km)

EASTBOURNE – BEACHY HEAD – BIRLING GAP
SEVEN SISTERS SHEEP FARM – EAST DEAN – FRISTON
JEVINGTON – FILCHING MANOR MOTOR MUSEUM
POLEGATE – STONE CROSS – EASTBOURNE

1. Eastbourne Pier to Beachy Head ($3\frac{1}{2}$mile/5.8km)

Leave Eastbourne Pier westward along Grand Parade for Beachy Head. Continue along Upper Dukes Drive turning left where signposted Beachy Head. There are several car parks and free parking areas available here.

Toilets and refreshments available.

2. Beachy Head to Birling Gap ($2\frac{3}{4}$ mile/4.6km)

Continue along the coast road to Birling Gap where there is a large car park beside the row of cottages.

Toilets and refreshments available.

3. Birling Gap to Seven sisters Sheep Centre ($\frac{3}{4}$mile/1.3km)

Leave Birling Gap by the road to the left for East Dean. In $\frac{3}{4}$ mile the entrance to the Seven Sisters Sheep Centre is on the right where there is free parking.

Toilets and refreshments available including picnic facilities.

4. Seven Sisters Sheep Centre to East Dean ($\frac{1}{2}$mile/0.8km)

Turn right out of the Seven Sisters Sheep Centre and continue into East Dean where there is a large free car park signposted left in $\frac{1}{2}$ mile.

Toilets and refreshments available.

5. East Dean to Friston ($\frac{3}{4}$mile/1.3km)

Turn left out of the car park and left again at the A259 signposted Seaford. Turn off left by Friston church where there is limited parking by the pond.

No toilets or refreshment facilities available here.

6. Friston to Jevington ($2\frac{1}{4}$mile/3.6km)

Cross the A259 signposted Jevington. Continue into the village where there is a car park off to the left just before the first of the houses.

Toilets and refreshments available at the Eight Bells public house in the village.

7. Jevington to Filching Manor Motor Museum $1^1/_4$mile/2.1km)

Turn left out of the car park and continue through the village. In $1^1/_4$mile the entrance to Filching Manor Motor Museum is on the right.

Toilets and refreshments are available.

8. Filching Manor Motor Museum to Polegate (2mile/3.3km)

Turn right out of the Motor Museum continuing through Wannock to the traffic lights. Keep straight ahead over the level crossing by Polegate railway station to the T-junction where you turn right. Through the traffic lights take the first turning left signposted cuckoo Trail where the car park is round to the left in Windsor Way.

There are no toilets or refreshment facilities available here although there are several public houses in the village.

9. Polegate to Stone Cross ($2^1/_4$mile/3.8km)

Return to the A27 and turn left. In $1^1/_2$mile (2.5km) turn right onto the B2104 signposted Eastbourne. At the crossroads in $^3/_4$mile (1.3km) turn left where there is limited parking in a layby just past the church.

Toilets and refreshments available at the Red Lion public house on the crossroads.

10. Stone Cross to Eastbourne ($4^1/_4$mile/7.1km)

Return to the crossroads keeping straight across signposted Eastbourne. In $1^1/_4$mile (2km) turn right at the Langney Centre and in a further $^3/_4$mile (1.3km) follow the signs for Seafront and Sovereign Centre. At the Sovereign Centre turn along Royal Parade past Fort Fun, the Butterfly Centre and the Redoubt back to the Pier to conclude the tour.

POINTS OF INTEREST DURING THE TOUR

1. Beachy Head

This 575 feet (175m) sea cliff might not be the highest in Britain but it is certainly the best known and most visited.

The name "Beachy" is derived from the French 'beau chef' meaning beautiful headland. The Head, along with its neighbouring Seven Sisters cliff top, is protected from development and much of the coastline and inlying area is jointly owned by the National Trust and the Forestry Commission. Eastbourne Corporation bought 1600 hectares in 1924 and in 1957 acquired a further 40 hectares at Whitebread Hole as a gift. The National Trust owns over 250 hectares of the Seven Sisters while the Forestry Commission owns Friston Forest north of the A259.

The red-banded lighthouse built in 1902 is much photographed against the white chalk cliffs and it replaced the Belle Tout lighthouse which can still be seen further along the cliff top.

On top of Beachy Head, in the small octagonal brick enclose, is all that remains of a Lloyd's signal station which was built in 1886.

Mesolithic and Neolithic remains have been found in the area proving that man inhabited the Downs since about 12000BC.

A public house and cafeteria provide refreshments and there are also toilet facilities here.

Public Transport: Service 3 from Eastbourne to Beachy Head operated by Eastbourne Buses and South Coast Buses every 30 minutes during the day (no evening service) every day, Sunday included.

Walk: A circular walk (9mile/15km). *See page 49.*

Beachy Head and lighthouse.

2. Birling Gap

There is a car park here, a public house, a few cottages huddled on the hillside and a row of coastguard cottages which survive from the nineteenth century and little else save for a beach and access to magnificent coastal scenery – the beginning of the famous Seven Sisters.

The cliffs from Eastbourne as far as Seaford have been defined as the Sussex Heritage Coast and are some of the finest sea-cliffs in Britain.

The sea has eroded much of the cliffs along this stretch of the coastline, even some of the coastguard cottages have fallen victim to its remorseless pounding, and it was because of the elements the old Belle Tout lighthouse became redundant.

Built in 1832 by Jack Fuller, a well known Sussex eccentric, it became fog bound perched high on the cliffs for six months of the year and therefore rendered practically useless. It was replaced by the present red-banded lighthouse at the foot of Beachy Head and Belle Tout was converted into a private dwelling before the war and given to Eastbourne Corporation. It has been used several times in film locations and advertising campaigns.

A public house provides refreshments and toilet facilities.

Public Transport: Birling Gap is not served by any public transport.

Walk: A circular walk (3mile/5km) begins from Birling Gap car park linking part of the Seven Sisters headland with the National Trust village of Crowlink. (See page 58).

The Seven Sisters and Cuckmere Haven from Birling Gap.

3. Seven Sisters Sheep Centre

A family run farm with over 30 different breeds of sheep on display, some rare breeds no longer seen on modern sheep farms.

Set in an historic seventeenth century flint barn there are lots of young farm animals to feed and hold including pigs, goats, calves, rabbits and chicks.

In summer there are regular demonstrations of sheep milking, cheese making, shearing and spinning while a wide variety of sheep orientated gifts and produce are on sale in the farm shop, including yoghurts and cheese.

Light refreshments are available in the Tea Room or picnic facilities are provided. There are toilets and free parking available. Admission charge.

Hours of Opening: Mid March - mid September (with restricted opening during May) 2.00 p.m.-5.00 p.m. Weekdays, 11.00 a.m.-5.00 p.m. Weekends and School Holidays.

Public Transport: There is no public transport serving the Sheep Centre but it is only 1/2mile (0.8km) from East Dean which is served by Service 712 Eastbourne - Brighton route.

4. East Dean

Jonathon Darby came to be vicar here in 1706 at the church that was started by Saxons finished by Normans and had an abundance of unnamed graves in its churchyard, victims of the merciless rocks between Eastbourne and Birling Gap.

There was no lighthouse then and in an effort to save the appalling loss of life every time there was a storm Darby hollowed out a cave in the cliffs well above the high-tide line and constructed a sloping tunnel with steps leading up from the beach. Whenever there was a storm he would shelter in his cave hanging a lamp outside to guide any shipwrecked sailor to safety.

Belle Tout lighthouse did this work to better avail a century later and Beachy Head lighthouse now ensures the safety of practically all shipping passing the coast today but Jonathon Darby will be forever remembered in East Dean even though his cave, tunnel and steps have long since been washed away with the tides.

The church registers tell another interesting story, that of the Payne sisters who were buried here in 1796. One sister was taken ill and struck dumb as she cried out for her fit sister to join her. Within half an hour she too was taken ill and both sisters died the following morning.

The village also boasts to have the first cable office connecting Britain with the continent which is still evident. Its wires were carried by telegraph poles across the Downs connecting with an undersea cable at Birling Gap.

Birling Manor nearby was the home of the Gurneys whose daughter married William Bardoff in 1257. The Bardoffs had a knack of marrying rich heiresses it seems but equally had the misfortune for backing the wrong side in parliamentary affairs.

The Tiger Inn, on the green, was probably so named in error. Taken from the Bardoff coat of arms depicting a leopard, the landlord four centuries ago mistook the identity of the beast having never seen either.

The walls of the church are three feet thick, the timbers of the roof are fifteenth century and the pulpit with its handsome canopy and rich carved panels is thought to have been made by a village craftsman shortly after the time Shakespeare died. But it is the font that has the best tale to tell, for half of it is old and the other half new; half of it has been up in the roof and half of it down in the sea.

One day some men on the roof found the older western half under one of the beams up there. For the other half they went down to the beach at low tide and dug up a boulder from under Beachy Head. On it they completed the Norman design of the bowl which has two bands of

The Green, East Dean, showing the Tiger Inn on the right.

moulding round the top and bottom with circles linking up between. Then the two halves were joined together as one.

Another prized possession is in a glass case on the wall; a pewter chalice and plate found in a priest's coffin. They are the earliest known type and there are only three sets like them in Sussex. They were buried here soon after King John signed Magna Carta.

The Tiger public house provides refreshments and toilet facilities.

Public Transport: Service 712 from Eastbourne to Brighton passes through East Dean operated by Brighton and Hove Buses and South Coast Buses every 30 minutes during the day, hourly during the evening and on Sundays.

5. Friston

The name Friston is probably derived from the Saxon landowner 'Fritha' who had his 'Tun' or enclosure nearby; hence 'Fritha's tun'.

The church, which stands by a pond, looks out one way over the English Channel and the other over the beautiful Weald of Sussex beyond Friston Forest. Its oldest part dates back to the reign of Edward the Confessor (AD 1042) and in the wall by the door is its most interesting feature – a tiny Saxon window, blocked up and made long before the use of glass was known. The original doorway is also built up giving a clue as to the history of the nave.

The Selwyns, who lived at Friston Place in Shakespeare's day, are bestowed in the transept; a large family of 38 issue and yet remarkably they still died out of existence!

The parish registers, written on parchment, begin in 1546 and give account of several sidelights on parochial history, such as when fire destroyed East Dean vicarage in 1665 it was the Selwyns who provided a replacement, giving what is now known as the Old Parsonage, asking only in return that a sermon in memory of the Selwyn family be preached annually in Friston church.

Entrance to the churchyard is through a curious tapsell or pintle gate (coffin gate) which is hung on a central axis and can be opened either way. Such gates are not unusual in this part of Sussex for there is another at Jevington and also at Kingston near Lewes.

What is unusual is the stark wooden cross in the churchyard bearing the simple words 'washed ashore', testament to the uncertain moods of the sea along this coast.

The distinguished composer Frank Bridge (1879-1941) lies in the graveyard; he was teacher to Benjamin Britten and deputised for Sir Henry Wood at the 'Proms'.

There are no toilets or refreshment facilities here.

Public Transport: Service 712 from Eastbourne to Brighton operated by Brighton and Hove Buses and South Coast Buses passes Friston pond every 30 minutes during the day, hourly in the evening and on Sundays.

Friston Church and Dewpond.

6. Jevington

The 'tun of Geofa's people', Jevington is of Saxon origin though never seems to have grown very much over the centuries. Nevertheless it is a pleasant little place with an interesting church which dates back to the early tenth century though there are traces of Roman bricks in the window arches of its fine tower. Some twelfth century Norman work has been masked somewhat by the efforts of an 1873 restoration which is a great pity for the splendid tower has been altered drastically!

Inside the church the Tudor roof is worthy of mention as is the fourteenth century font, but the most impressive possession is the fragment of sculpture as old as the tower which is set in the wall above the door. It is apparently an image of Christ thrusting a staff into a serpent's mouth, a crude Saxon interpretation of victory over evil. It was found only 200 years ago having long been buried under the floor.

In the churchyard is a tapsell gate on its central axis similar to the one at Friston only this specimen is even more curious having a stile incorporated in it.

The author photographed by the 'curious' tapsell gate, Jevington Church.

A fairly recent memorial in the churchyard near the south door is sculpted in bronze and is of a fully rigged frigate in great detail. It is to the memory of a Liverpool ship owner.

Other tombs in the graveyard were often used by smugglers in the eighteenth century to hide their contraband. The leader of one gang was James Pettit, otherwise known as Jevington Jigg, although he had several other aliases such as Jack Jigg, John Pettit, Wilson, Morgan, Gibbs and Williams to mention but a few. He was henchman to a tailor, horse thief and highwayman and was keeper of the local public house from which most of their infamous activities originated.

The nocturnal activities of Jevington Jigg soon attracted the attention of the authorities and his chequered career kept him in trouble with the law for several years. He was transported for seven years for stealing two hams but only served part of the sentence then, in the summer of 1799, he was convicted of horse stealing at Salisbury and condemned to death. The sentence was later transmuted to 14 years at Botany Bay and there, in all probability, he died for nothing more was heard of him.

It seems the parsons at the church were akin to the smuggling rackets, either actively involved or turned a blind eye to what was going on and Nat Collier, whose curious memorial is in the north-west corner of the chancel, was probably one of them. It says he died on March 1 169½, so presumably nobody was quite sure in which year.

The Eight Bells public house may well have figured in the dealings of Jevington Jigg. At his time it was a private house but there were underground passages leading to it, one from Thorpe House and another from a house called Jiggs, which could very well have been the home of James Pettit. Around 1810 it was sold to John Gorring, a brewer from Seaford, and it was immediately granted a licence and became known as the Eight Bells. Exactly why this name was chosen is a mystery for the church of St Andrew has only two bells in its tower.

Today the Eight Bells provides refreshment and toilet facilities and the Hungry Monk is well known in the area for its restaurant. There is also a tea room in the village.

Public Transport: Jevington is connected to Eastbourne and Polegate by service 213 operated by South Coast Buses on Tuesdays and Thursdays only. There are only two buses on each of these days allowing about 3¼ hours stay between each of them.

Walk: There is a superb walk starting from Jevington: a continuation of the South Downs Way to the Long Man and back through Folkington along the Wealdway (7mile/11.6km). (See page 61).

7. Filching Manor Motor Museum

The Foulk or Folk People landed at Folkestone around AD600 and raped and pillaged their way up the coast of England founding ffulching (Filching), Folkington and Fulking near Brighton. Four centuries later, during a northern migration, they founded Folkingham in Lincolnshire along with other places of the 'Foulk' ilk.

The Foulkes-Halbard family of Filching Manor originated with the invading Saxons of the sixth and seventh centuries and the Manor House was certainly mentioned in the Domesday Survey although records show it was first mentioned in the Saxon Chronicles dating back to AD810. Its oldest door is still in daily use and it has smoke blackened oak rafters dating back from the days before fireplaces. Inside is a magnificent example of Medieval construction with its early stained glass, minstrel gallery and extensive panelling.

Today it houses a mass of motor memorabilia dating back over the first century of motoring including a restoration of the K3 Hydroplane world record breaker of 1937 and 1938 which was driven by Sir Malcolm Campbell at speeds in excess of 130mph. Also on display is the prototype K7 boat built for the successful BBC film "Across the Lake" about the life of Donald Campbell.

Toilets and refreshments are available here.

Hours of Opening: Between Easter and the end of September from 10.30 a.m.-4.30 p.m. Thursday to Sunday and Bank Holidays. There is an admission charge.

Public Transport: Served by service 213 from Eastbourne and Polegate and operated by South Coast Buses on Tuesdays and Thursdays only. There are only two buses on each of these days allowing about 3 hours stay between them. Passengers may have to board and alight at Wannock Village Hall which is approximately 1/2 mile from the entrance to the Motor Museum and time to cover this distance should be allowed for in each direction.

8. Polegate

The first recorded reference to Polegate was in 1563 when it was known as Powlegate Corner. In 1579 it became Poolgate while in 1620 a survey mentions a rivulet called the Broughton Streame leading from Paul Gate to Jevington. A toll gate is known to have existed near the present crossroads and this could well have been owned by a man named Paul which could account for the survey's findings.

In 1780 the Estate of Polegate was held by the Swaine family but sixty years later there were only seven houses in the area so it was not of much significance. Then came the railways and the population began to increase to an extent that it became known as a railwayman's village. By 1873 there were 50 houses and the parish church was built the following year. It has a fine open timbered roof and has a brick facing with reproduction windows in the thirteenth and fourteenth century style.

To the north of the village stands Otteham Court within an old walled garden. It occupies the site of a grange of the Premonstratentian canons before they moved to Lamberhurst and built Bayham Abbey. The site was granted to them in the twelfth century during the reign of Henry II and its most interesting feature is the chapel of the canons. Of early fourteenth century it retains a gabled sedilia and piscina and two small windows of the same date.

Nearby is Sayerlands which was also part of the monastic grange, being a farm of the canons. It dates from the sixteenth century with superimposed eighteenth century front and three bay windows.

Public Transport: Polegate is served by British Rail Network SouthEast and with regular trains from Eastbourne throughout the day, hourly on Sundays. Numerous buses operate from Eastbourne to Brighton, Hailsham etc, all passing through Polegate on a regular basis daily.

9. Stone Cross

The Stone Cross stands in the churchyard on the crossroads of this rather uninteresting village save for the windmill which is situated about 1/4mile from the junction along the Pevensey road.

Built in 1876 from bricks made in an adjacent brickfield it has unusually shaped wheel windows and was fitted with a fluted beehive cap, lofty fan tail and staging protected by an outsized storm door. it carried four double-shuttered sweeps each 5'6" wide giving a total span of 68 feet. Its original intention was to work four pairs of stones but when the millwright installed the extensive interior fittings and machinery in 1877 only three pairs of stones were positioned.

All the ironwork was founded in Lewes and swung into position from the mast of an old sailing ship set well into the ground alongside the mill building and used as a hoist.

It was originally known as Blackness Mill because the tower and cap were painted white in stark contrast to the black painted roundel which extended well beyond the diametrical limits of the mill base.

In 1925 two of the sweeps blew off in a gale and were never replaced but nevertheless the mill continued operating for a further ten years with only the two sweeps quite successfully.

During World War II the Army used the mill as an observation post after which it then returned to private ownership.

In 1962 planning permission was granted to convert the mill for residential use but in 1975 it was restored to full working order but it is no longer open to the public and stands testament to better days gone by.

Parking near the mill is difficult as it is now situated in the middle of private dwellings but it is accessible on foot.

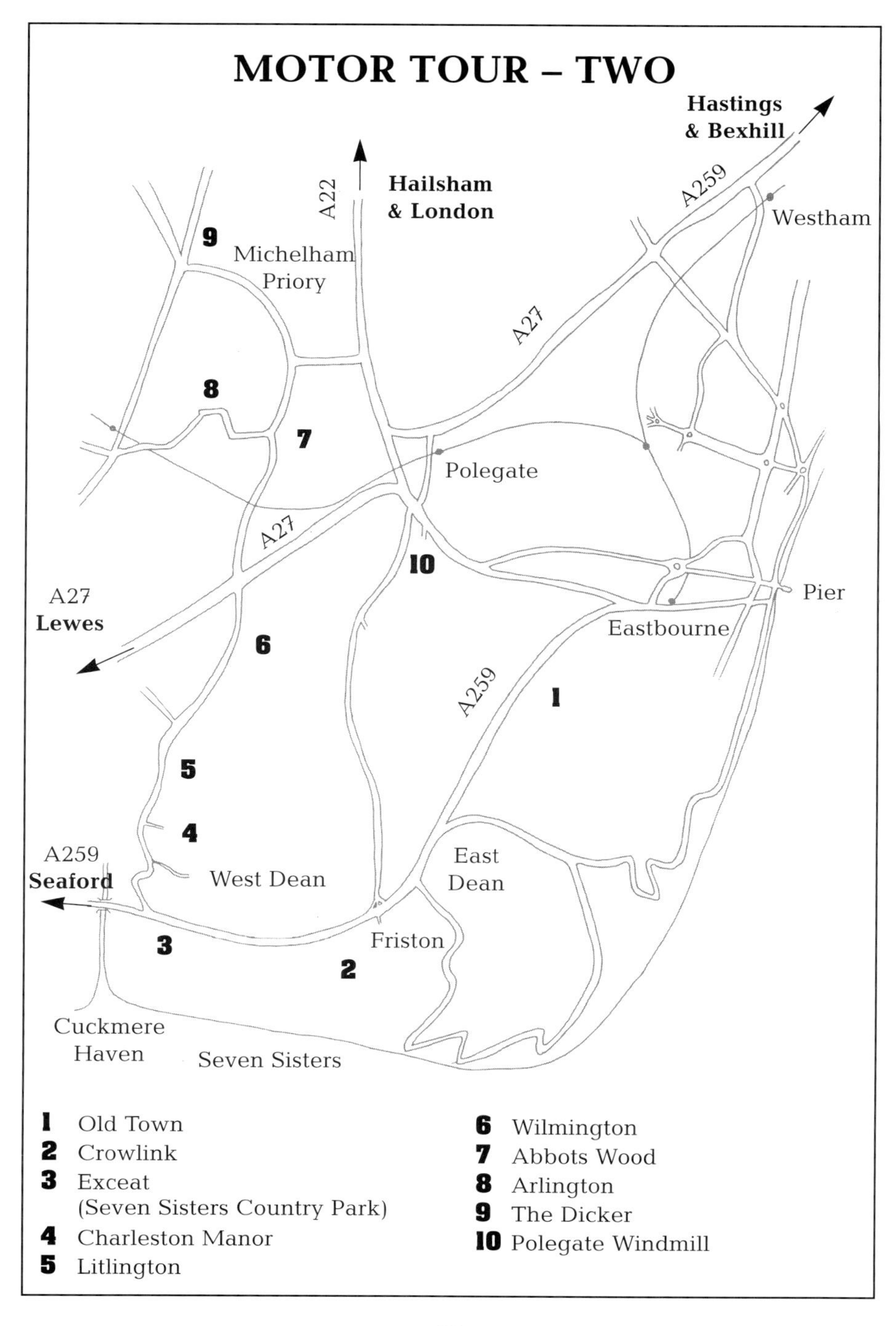
MOTOR TOUR – TWO
Hastings & Bexhill
A22
Hailsham & London
A259
Westham
9
Michelham Priory
A27
8
7
Polegate
A27
10
Pier
A27
Lewes
Eastbourne
6
A259
1
5
4
East Dean
A259
Seaford
West Dean
Friston
3
2
Cuckmere Haven
Seven Sisters
1 Old Town
2 Crowlink
3 Exceat (Seven Sisters Country Park)
4 Charleston Manor
5 Litlington
6 Wilmington
7 Abbots Wood
8 Arlington
9 The Dicker
10 Polegate Windmill

MOTOR TOUR – TWO (32mile/51km)

EASTBOURNE (OLD TOWN & TOWNER ART GALLERY AND MUSEUM) - CROWLINK – EXCEAT (SEVEN SISTERS COUNTRY PARK/LIVING WORLD & WEST DEAN) – CHARLESTON MANOR LITLINGTON – WILMINGTON – ABBOTS WOOD – ARLINGTON THE DICKER – MICHELHAM PRIORY – POLEGATE WINDMILL EASTBOURNE

1. Eastbourne Pier to Old Town ($1^1/_2$mile/2.3km)

Leave Eastbourne Pier following the A2021 to London. At the large roundabout keep left following the A259 to Brighton. At the Upperton Road traffic lights turn right then left soon afterwards where signposted Brighton. Turn left up Borough Lane – opposite the Lamb Inn just before the church – where there is ample on street parking.

Toilets and refreshments available.

2. Old Town to Crowlink ($3^3/_4$mile/6km)

Turn right along Vicarage Road back to the A259 where turn left up the steep hill past Eastbourne Golf Club. Keep ahead through East Dean turning left at Friston church and pond signposted Crowlink. Continue for $^1/_4$mile along an unmade road to the National Trust car park at Crowlink.

There are no toilets or refreshments available at Crowlink.

3. Crowlink to Exceat (Country Park) ($2^1/_2$mile/4km)

Return to the A259 and turn left. The car park at Cuckmere Haven is on the left opposite the Living World.

Toilets and refreshments are available.

4. Exceat (Country Park) to Charleston Manor (1mile/1.6km)

Turn left onto the A259 and right almost immediately signposted West Dean/Litlington. The entrance to Charleston Manor is in 1mile on the right.

Toilets and refreshments are available.

5. Charleston Manor to Litlington ($^3/_4$mile/1.2km)

Turn right out of Charleston Manor and continue into Litlington where there is no parking except the Plough and Harrow public house car park where there are toilets and refreshments available.

6. Litlington to Wilmington ($2^1/_4$mile/3.6km)

Carry on past Lullington Church (where there is no parking readily available) to Wilmington where the car park for the Priory and Long Man is signposted to the left.

Toilets in the car park. Refreshments at the Giants Rest public house further into the village.

7. Wilmington to Abbots Wood ($2^1/_2$mile/4km)

Left out of the Priory car park and through the village to the A27. Cross straight over signposted Abbots Wood, turning right at the T-junction then right again into the Nature Reserve where there is unlimited parking.

Toilets available but refreshments at the Old Oak public house further along the approach road to Abbots Wood.

8. Abbots Wood to Arlington ($1^1/_4$mile/2km)

Turn left out of the Nature Reserve into Arlington. At the Yew Tree public house keep straight ahead for the church and car park off to the left.

Toilets and refreshments available.

9. Arlington to The Dicker (5mile/8km)

Return to the Yew Tree public house and turn right signposted Seaford/Lewes. Follow the road under the railway bridge to the crossroads where turn right signposted Dicker. After $2^3/_4$mile (4.6km) turn right signposted Arlington/Michelham Priory. The Dicker church is on this corner and the entrance to Michelham Priory is a little further along on the left.

Toilets and refreshments are available.

10. The Dicker to Polegate Windmill (6mile/10km)

Turn left out of Michelham Priory car park keeping ahead as far as the A22. Traffic here has to turn left as far as the next roundabout where double back on the opposite lanes of the dual carriageway signposted Eastbourne. Keep ahead at both sets of traffic lights but about $^1/_4$mile (0.3km) past the second set (at Polegate crossroads) turn off right to visit the Windmill where there is limited parking.

There are no toilets or refreshments available here.

11. Polegate Windmill to Eastbourne Pier (5¼mile/8.6km)

Return to the A22 turning right. Follow all A2021 signs to Eastbourne back to the Pier.

POINTS OF INTEREST ON THE TOUR

1. Old Town

The spring that became the Bourne Stream upon which the early settlements depended has its source here. The oldest inhabitants favoured a holding to the east of the Bourne Stream and so the present name of Eastbourne developed.

At the time of the Norman Conquest the Manor of Bourne was handed to Robert, Count of Mortain, the Conqueror's half brother. By the time of the Domesday Survey, twenty years later, the Manor had become an established hundred – a political area of no specific size which usually enveloped several parishes. In the case of Bourne the Manor had a church, watermill and sixteen saltpans. It was unique in being a parish and hundred as one; albeit a relatively large parish but one of the smallest hundreds covering only 5000 acres including 3560 acres of ploughland.

Parish Church of St Mary

Although there was an early church here its site is unknown for the parish church of St Mary was begun in 1160 with the first phase finished thirty years later. It was built with Caen stone shipped from Normandy. Its architectural glory is the Norman chancel arch and with a modern east window shining through is a delight to the eye. Another window in one of the aisles is over 500 years old, of Flemish glass and depicting the Crucifixion and what appears to be pictures of the Prodigal Son and Solomon receiving the Queen of Sheba. A fine painting hanging on one of the walls is of the Descent from the Cross.

By the altar is a little of the old screen and in the chancel four or five massive old screens. Facing the stone sedilia is the Easter Sepulchre with Norman columns on either side on which the masons left their little fishes trademark almost 900 years ago.

A marble tablet on the wall to Davies Gilbert is of interest. He was the son of a Cornish curate and he loved geology. As a boy he knew Humphrey Davy and invited him home to read some of his books which aided his invention of the famous safety lamp. He also knew Richard Trevithick and made calculations to help him with his engine and he helped Thomas Telford too by reckoning the length of the chains he would need for his famous bridge across the Menai Straits.

In its churchyard is a sundial that has been marking the hours for almost 300 years and the old cross between the church wall and the Lamb Inn has been around for many more centuries before that. It was brought here from Cornwall in the days when there was nothing but a horse to bring it and it is very rare for it is believed there are only five others like it.

St Mary's Church, Old Town, Eastbourne.

The Lamb Inn

It began life as home to a band of monks and was converted to an inn at the time of the Reformation. It has a crypt or vaulted cellar in the Early English style but the whole place has been altered in some detail since then. There was a particularly heavy restoration around 1912 when the exterior walls were covered with white painted stucco without a sign of the many beams in evidence today.

During the Napoleonic wars the area was full of soldiers and the Lamb was in the midst of social activities. Its assembly room and ballroom have always been in great demand but a more serious meeting was held in May 1852 when a Mr Darling gave a lecture on spiritualism and memorism. During proceedings there was a violent thunderstorm that the audience was so convinced it was a manifestation of Satan that they ran from the inn for their lives. Todays' patrons hopefully leave in a more orderly manner!

The Lamb Inn, Old Town.

Towner Art Gallery and Museum

The Manor that now houses the Towner Art Gallery and Museum was built in the 1770s and was bought by Charles Gilbert from Sir Stephen Lushington in 1792. Known as the Gilbert Manor House it remained in the Gilbert family until 1922 when the house and grounds were sold to Eastbourne Corporation. The following year the Towner Art Gallery was housed in the Manor and opened to the public. Sixty years later a local museum was added to the Art Gallery depicting the history of Eastbourne through the ages from prehistoric times to present day. The Victorian kitchen display features two old cooking ranges from the original Manor.

Hours of Opening: Wednesday to Saturday 10.00 a.m.-5.00 p.m.; Sunday and Bank Holidays 2.00 p.m.-5.00 p.m. The Gardens are open daily with free access. There is an admission charge to the Museum and Art Gallery. Toilets and refreshments are available.

Public Transport: Service 712 from Eastbourne to Brighton passes through Old Town operated by Brighton and Hove Buses and South Coast Buses every 30 minutes during the day, hourly in the evenings and on Sundays.

2. Crowlink

The "Hill of Crows" was once the home of E. Nesbit who wrote 'The Railway Children'. Its buildings nestle snugly in the valley that was once a working estate but now most are private dwellings or holiday homes. The cellars of Crowlink House are said to have stored "Genuine Crowlink", smuggled gin which fetched high prices in the nineteenth century. The last recorded skirmish near Crowlink between smugglers and excisemen was at Flagstaff Point in 1782 when two smugglers and one exciseman were killed.

There is no known record of the misfortunes that befell Simon Payn that forced him to leave Crowlink and accept the charity of Bayham Abbey, but the Abbot undertook to care for him and his family in 1290 for as long as they should live. His descendants must have encountered better fortune for they returned to Crowlink where they lived for several generations. Even today the name Payn is still to be found in this area of Sussex.

Crowlink hamlet.

There are no public toilets or refreshments available here.

Public Transport: Service 712 from Eastbourne to Brighton operated by Brighton and Hove Buses and South Coast Buses stops at Friston pond on the A259 every 30 minutes during the day, hourly in the evening and on Sunday. Crowlink is about 1/4mile (0.4km) down the unmade road as signposted.

Walk: A circular walk (7 1/2mile/12km) begins from the National Trust car park, through Crowlink to the cliff top path, then along part of the Seven Sisters to Cuckmere Haven and back through Friston Forest. (See page 65).

3. Exceat

Once this was quite an important little fishing village nestling near the mouth of the River Cuckmere, but repeated incursions by French raiding parties following the ravages of the Black Death in 1348-9 caused the population to decline to virtual extinction by the early sixteenth century. It was excavated between the two World Wars and the Sussex Archaeological Society have erected a tablet on the site of the old church.

The Saxons were obviously here for the River Cuckmere is named from a Saxon word meaning "flowing water" and it was much wider in their day too. Before that it was known as the River Exe from which the old village was named.

Today Cuckmere Haven is one of the few natural havens left in Britain, unspoilt by human development but left to allow nature to survive in its natural habitat. It is because of this the area has been designated a Country Park for the enjoyment of all.

Seven Sisters Country Park

For centuries the River Cuckmere meandered through the gap cut through the chalk cliffs between Haven Brow and Seaford Head. High tides regularly flooded the valley it created forming great mud flats which are now good feeding grounds for many species of birds including cormorants, redshank heron and mute swan. A lagoon which was created provides nesting for little and ringed plover on its shingle islands and the highest tides fill the creeks with sea water creating salt marshes in which hydrobia (tiny snails) live providing food for all the birds that feed here.

The Seven Sisters Country Park covers the lower part of the Cuckmere Valley and part of the Seven Sisters cliffs and is owned and managed by East Sussex County Council. A circular park trail begins at the car park and explanatory leaflets are available from the Park Centre which is housed in a converted eighteenth century barn on the opposite side of the A259. There is also a special "Valley Walk' for the disabled and wheelchair users.

Other facilities in the Country Park include cycling, canoeing, rowing, camping, fishing, swimming and horse riding, details of which can all be obtained from the Park Centre.

The Living World

Housed in adjacent barns to the Park Centre the Living World is a fascinating display of flora and fauna of the area including butterflies, insects, marine life and minerals. All parts of the exhibition are accessible to wheelchairs.

Hours of Opening: Easter to the end of October, 10.00 a.m.-5.00 p.m. Also open weekends and school holidays during the winter.

Free entry to the Park Centre. Admission charge to the Living World.

Toilets and refreshments available including picnic facilities in the Country Park.

Visitor Centre and car park, Seven Sisters Country Park.

West Dean

Alfred the Great owned a manor here and Asser, the monk who was to become a bishop and the King's biographer, was summoned to visit Alfred and recorded his royal welcome at West Dean. Until early last century a manor house stood in the centre of the village with only a dovecot and fragments of a wall remaining today. Whether this was Alfred's manor is speculative. What does remain, however, is maintained to being the oldest inhabited house in Sussex, probably Britain, for in part it dates back to 1220 with flint and stone walls two and a half feet thick and a stone spiral staircase. Most of the buildings in the village are noticeably built of flint.

The church of All Saints dates back to the Saxons, a slit in the window of the nave being attributed to their architecture. The nave, bell tower and round arch are all Norman but most of the rest is fourteenth century. Inside are two canopied tombs over 600 years old, one richly carved, and a robed magistrate of the Charles Stuart era kneeling with his veiled wife under an arch adorned with gilded cherubs. There are two modern busts, one of the painter Sir Oswald Birley and the other, by Epstein, of the 1st Viscount Waverley – better known as Sir John Anderson – a member of Churchill's War Cabinet, who lived in the village and is buried in the churchyard.

The Lamplands and Taperlands have long since disappeared from this astonishing place cradled in the midst of Friston Forest and all but lost to the outside world. They were the fields, the rents from which went to the church to pay for oil to keep a lamp burning above the altar and to buy tapers and candles for the interior.

Cars are discouraged from entering the village for there is no parking within. It is best to park either at the Country Park car park or one of the Friston Forest car parks and walk in. There is a surprising beauty about this tranquil place that is greatly enhanced by a gentle stroll around its interior for this is indeed a marvellous piece of unspoilt England.

Public Transport: Service 712 Eastbourne to Brighton route operated by Brighton and Hove Buses and South Coast Buses pass Seven Sisters Country Park every 30 minutes during the day, hourly in the evenings and on Sunday.

Walk: A 7¾mile (12.8km) walk begins from the Country Park and visits West Dean, Litlington and Alfriston before returning to Exceat along the bank of the River Cuckmere. *(See page 69).*

4. Charleston Manor

Of Norman origin and standing in beautiful gardens which are sometimes open to the public.

The Domesday Survey shows that the Manor was granted to Earl Warrene, the Conqueror's son-in-law, and it is later recorded that a Tudor wing was added to the original house and a Georgian front was built between 1710-30. The remains of a twelfth century manor house may still be seen in the grounds which also include a large tithe barn and walled gardens, but its prize possession is a dovecot, circular with a conical roof and walls two and a half feet thick. It has 350 nesting holes and a centrally hinged ladder which can be rotated to give access to all of them.

Sir Oswald Birley, the painter (1880-1952), bought Charleston Manor in 1931 commissioning architect Walter Godfrey to restore the building. The barn alongside the house became the portrait painter's studio doubling as a small theatre with a stage for actors and musicians and became the venue for the annual Charleston Festival.

Opposite the main entrance to Charleston Manor high on the side of Hindover (referred to as High and Over on the Ordnance Survey map) is an uninhibited view of the 90 foot-long **White Horse** carved in the chalk. It was carved out sometime during the nineteenth century, probably as a youthful prank, by James Pagden, his brother and a cousin. James Pagden was the father of Florence Pagden the historian who lived in nearby Alfriston.

Hours of Opening: The house is not open to the public but the gardens are on Sundays during the summer between 2.00 and 6.00 p.m.

Public Transport: The Cuckmere Community Bus (CCB) passes the entrance to Charleston Manor on TUESDAYS AND FRIDAYS only connecting with service 712 at the Seven Sisters Country Park (Exceat) and Seaford.

N.B. There is NO service to coincide with the gardens being open on Sunday. It is approximately 1mile (1.6km) from the Seven Sisters Country Park.

5. Litlington

A pretty little village of Saxon origin, its name meaning quite simply "Little Homestead".

It has the distinction of having the county's original tea gardens, for it was here that Mr Russell introduced the first at the turn of the century. They are becoming an increasing rarity these days but Litlington Tea Gardens are unique and a must to visit.

Mrs Maria Fitzherbert lived at Clapham House before she married George IV. The house is still here but is privately owned and not open to public view.

The church, a little way out of the village, was started by the Normans but finished virtually two centuries later, its windows framed with chalk. It has a low, small door in the North wall giving access to a winding stone staircase to the belfry and inside there are two lancet windows in the chancel richly ornated with glass thought to be fourteenth century depicting the figures of an angel, a winged lion and a golden eagle. The roof is built of ancient beams and the font dates back half a millenium.

Toilets and refreshments are available either at the Tea Gardens or the Plough and Harrow public house.

For the highly recommended detour to the charming and unique village of Alfriston, follow road signs to the village indicated shortly after leaving Litlington. (For further details see page 72).

Public Transport: The Cuckmere Community Bus (CCB) passes through Litlington on Tuesdays and Fridays only connecting with service 712 Eastbourne to Brighton route at Seven Sisters Country Park (Exceat).
N.B. The Tuesday service allows 2 hours stay in Litlington. On Fridays only one bus operates and there is NO return service.

Entrance to Litlington Tea Gardens.

6. Wilmington

The restored old buildings of Wilmington make this one of the most picturesque village streets in the county. But it is not only the village that attracts visitors in their thousands to this pretty part of Sussex, interesting though it is with its twelfth century church and old Priory ruins, for Wilmington is dominated by The Long Man, one of the most remarkable pieces of ancient craftsmanship anywhere in the world.

The largest chalk figure in England, The Long Man is as much a mystery today as he ever has been. Over 226 feet high and preserved with white painted concrete blocks 'his' origin remains unknown. Theory has it the Saxons made him a thousand years or more ago – though he could very well have been there a thousand years before that. Some say the monks of Wilmington made him; but the truth is nobody is certain how he came to be – a truly baffling figure, impressive and awe-inspiring with his two staves a little longer than himself.

The Long Man of Wilmington.

After the Norman Conquest the Manor of Wilmington became the property of the Benedictine Abbey of Grestain in Normandy. It was in the beginning of the twelfth century that the Priory was built as the headquarters of the Abbot of Grestain's representative in England and was intended to accommodate no more than two or three monks and

Wilmington Priory.

Yew Tree, Wilmington.

Arlington Reservoir

The reservoir was completed by Eastbourne Water Company in 1971 and supplies five million gallons of water daily. Private trout fishing is permissible and the reservoir when full holds 770 million gallons to a depth of 37 feet (11m). It was formed by cutting off a meander in the river and damming one end. The remains of prehistoric animals were found during its excavation and over 30,000 trees were planted on its completion including oak, birch, wild cherry, mountain ash and hawthorn.

8. Arlington

In line with other villages, Arlington was probably named after a Saxon landowner but the earliest written records is in the Churchwarden's Accounts for the years 1455-1479 which are preserved in the British Museum. They refer to the fact that the church had 30 cows which were let to farmers who paid for them in beeswax (2lbs per cow per annum) to supply lights for the shrine.

The church of St Pancras is one of the most interesting in the county having specimens of architecture from early Saxon times, including some Roman bricks presumably a legacy of the Roman road that once passed through the village.

The small window above the porch is Saxon and there is other Saxon work at the outside corners of the nave. It is believed an early Saxon church stood on the ground that once contained other buildings which had been burnt to the ground for evidence of charred remains has been found beneath the floor of the present church.

The Chapel is early Norman (1066-1090) with lancet windows and good examples of "dog tooth" ornament on the pillars. The stone coffin lids placed against the walls were taken from the chapel floor.

The aisle and tower are of the "Transitional Period" (1190-1245) while the roof arcade, east window and arches are dated 1245-1360. No part of the church is of later date than the Reformation.

The walls of the nave have traces of mural decoration belonging to two periods; the "roses and crosses" pattern being fourteenth century while the Elizabethan texts were superimposed in the seventeenth and eighteenth centuries.

At the end of the nineteenth century the church had fallen into a sorry state of repair – 'Worse than any other church in England' was how the Bishop described it and it underwent a major restoration accounting for its noble appearance today. During the restoration the present screen and chancel seats were made of timber taken from the old tower.

The church contains two great treasures. The jar in the glass case in the Chapel is a medieval food storage jar dating back to the thirteenth century. It may be the only specimen of its kind in Sussex and it was discovered under the floor, embedded in dark gravelly sand when the Tower was being strengthened between 1890/6. The second treasure is a twelfth century wooden chest, rough cut from a tree.

There are no shops in the village and only 45 houses in close proximity to the church.

Public Transport: The Cuckmere Community Bus (CCB) stops at the Yew Tree public house each Wednesday en route from Berwick Station (connecting with British Rail's service from Eastbourne). The service allows a 2 hour stay before the return bus to Berwick Station.

9. The Dicker

It seems to have been dominated most of this century by one man and an institution.

In the early days of the century it was Horatio Bottomley, MP who was squire of the village and there are still some old folk surviving who remember him with affection. For all that he was a rogue and a scoundrel who loved women and making money. An orphan, he made a fortune through newspapers and publishing for he was a financial wizard, brilliant orator and prize swindler. He rigged competitions, fixed lotteries and in 1922 appeared at the Old Bailey on 24 different fraudulent charges for which he was found guilty and sent to prison for seven years. That was his undoing, for he came out of prison a broken man and died four years later penniless.

During his heyday he built much of the village and bought up much of what was there already for the great wealth he amassed was not used only for his own purpose. He was a very generous man – he could afford to be – and built himself a mansion which had the only telephone in the village and then allowed everyone else to use it. He threw lavish parties, even persuaded the railway company to build the station at Berwick so his cronies could get easy access from London to attend. The Dicker, the mansion home he was so proud of, is now St Bedes public school which is now repeating Bottomley's process of buying up most of the village in its expansion.

The church is quite modern, being built in the middle of the last century on the site of a medieval fairground beside which is the remains of an ancient highway leading from Lewes to Battle (to the left of the White House on the corner of the present crossroads). In spite of this it contains much of interest, none more so than the superb east window to the memory of seven men who died for their country, their names being inscribed in it.

The font is old and was brought in from an unknown source. The base it stands on is new and was made purposely to support it. Behind it, on the wall, are details of an Elizabethan flagon which was given to the church by Margaret Lawrie in 1843. It was sold for £11,000 to form a trust which has since financed the church that now serves only a handful of congregation. This too will most probably be taken over by St Bedes once the coffers from the trust fund is gone.

The only other treasure remaining is the Bottomley Bible, presented to the church by the great man and in regular use until recently.

On the wall is a tablet relating to Owen Vidal, first incumbent of the church, who after only a few years service went to Africa to become Bishop of Sierra Leone before dying at the age of 35.

Public Transport: The Cuckmere Community Bus (CCB) runs Wednesday and Friday from Berwick Station (connecting with British Rail's service from Eastbourne). The Wednesday service does not coincide with Michelham Priory's opening times but the Friday service allows a visit of 2 hours.

10. Michelham Priory

Set within a beautiful seven acre island setting Michelham Priory has been rightfully described as a glorious piece of England and the loveliest stretch of the River Cuckmere.

The very name Michelham is Anglo-Saxon meaning "a large piece of land in a river bend".

Founded in 1229 by Gilbert de l'Aigle the Augustinian Priory of the Holy Trinity at Michelham housed between five and ten canons who through the careful management of their lands financed the running of the Priory. Religious houses were expected to provide hospitality to travellers whether rich or poor and in 1283 the Archbishop of Canterbury stayed as did King Edward I and his retinue in 1302.

Michelham was dissolved in 1537 and sold by the Crown in 1556. After a couple of quick changes in ownership it became a gentleman's residence before passing to Thomas Sackville in 1601 in whose family it remained for 300 years.

During the seventeenth and eighteenth centuries it was converted into a farm and in November 1896 James Eglington Anderson Gwynne of Folkington Manor bought the Priory beginning a programme of restoration until his death in 1915. Ten years later the Priory was sold again to Richard Beresford-Wright who restored the house further until a disastrous fire in December 1927 destroyed the Tudor Wing. In the 1930's the lawns and gardens were extended and the house was opened to the public for the first time a few days each year.

By May 1940 Sussex was expecting a German invasion and the Beresford-Wrights left the Priory and Canadian troops moved in. A plan for the Dieppe raid of August 1942 was drawn on the wall of the gatehouse where it remains to this day.

In 1958 the Priory was sold again with the proviso that it was preserved for posterity and the following year it was given, in trust, to the Sussex Archaeological Society who have continued to restore the gatehouse, repair the house and convert the mill back to full working order.

Hours of Opening: Daily March-October 11.00 a.m.-5.30 p.m.; Sundays in March and November 11.00 a.m.-4.00 p.m. Admission charge. Toilets and refreshments.

Public Transport: No public transport passes the Priory. The Cuckmere Community Bus (CCB) visits The Dicker (see 9).

Medieval gatehouse – Michelham Priory

11. Polegate Windmill

Polegate Windmill.

The mill was built in 1817 for Joseph Seymour. It stands 54 feet high and is 21 feet round at the base having four sweeps or sails which were designed to work two pairs of stones.

The mill worked by wind until 1943 when it was converted to become electrically driven until its closure in 1962.

It was purchased by the Eastbourne Civic Society in 1965 so that it could be preserved as an industrial monument and after extensive restoration work was officially opened to the public by the Society's president, His Grace the Duke of Devonshire, two years later. It is the only tower mill in East Sussex which is open to the public.

The ground floor and storeroom have been converted into a museum of milling memorabilia with displays and models helping to evoke an understanding of milling procedures.

Hours of Opening: Sundays and Bank Holiday afternoons between Easter Sunday and the end of September and on each Wednesday afternoon in August. Admission charge. No toilets or refreshments available.

Public Transport: Polegate is served by British Rail Network SouthEast with regular trains from Eastbourne throughout the day, hourly on

Sundays. The windmill is about ten minutes walk from Polegate Station. Numerous buses operate from Eastbourne to Brighton, Hailsham, etc, all passing through Polegate on a regular basis daily.

The Cuckoo Trail

The railway was first laid from Polegate to Hailsham in 1849 but it took thirty more years to extend it to Heathfield and Eridge. It was named the Cuckoo Line by the railwaymen because by local tradition the first cuckoo of spring was released each year at Heathfield Fair. The line was well used until 1961 when, in line with Dr Beeching's closures, it fell under the axe and the last passenger train ran in 1968.

Start of the Cuckoo Trail.

In 1981 Wealden District Council and East Sussex County Council bought the line and allowed it to be used as a public trail but little money was spent on the project and it fell into dereliction. Ten years later the present project was started in conjunction with Sustrans, a charity specialising in converting disused railway tracks, and the 10 mile stretch (16.6km) from Polegate to Heathfield was opened in 1993.

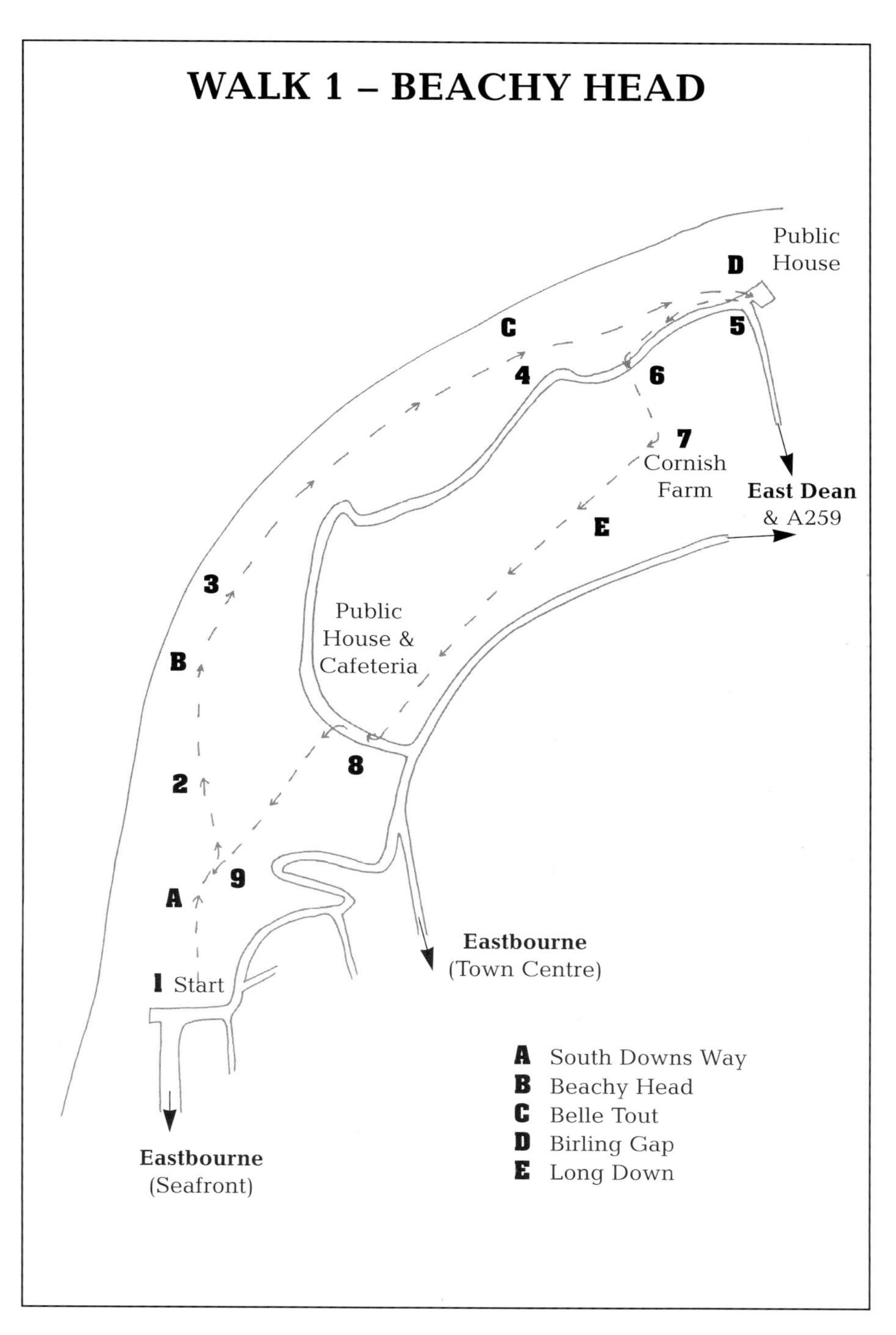
WALK 1 – BEACHY HEAD
Public House
D
C
5
4
6
7
Cornish Farm
East Dean
& A259
E
3
Public House & Cafeteria
B
8
2
9
A
Eastbourne
(Town Centre)
1 Start
Eastbourne
(Seafront)
A South Downs Way
B Beachy Head
C Belle Tout
D Birling Gap
E Long Down

WALK 1 – BEACHY HEAD

Parking:	At the western end of the Promenade by Holywell Retreat
Map Reference:	Landranger 199 grid reference 600971
Distance:	9 miles (15km)
Time to Allow:	4$^1/_2$ hours
Terrain:	Steep ascent and descent to start and finish the walk otherwise across undulating downland
Toilets/Refreshments:	Beachy Head and Birling Gap
Route:	Eastbourne–Beachy Head – Belle Tout – Birling Gap – Cornish Farm – Long Down – Eastbourne

Arguably the finest stretch of sea cliffs in Britain begin this walk to Beachy Head, its most famous headland and lighthouse. An exhilarating walk next to Belle Tout, the old lighthouse the present one replaced, before descending to Birling Gap where there are refreshments available. The return route sets off below Belle Tout before turning off towards Cornish Farm and then along Long Down back to Eastbourne.

Directions:

1. *Begin with a steep climb, up some steps and then on to an acorn marker post (the symbol of a Long Distance Footpath)* **(A)** *where fork right then left at the second post.*
2. *Follow the waymarkers along a track as far as an open clearing where keep left at the concrete footpath sign along a narrow path to Beachy Head* **(B).** *The deep hollow seaward side is Whitebread Hole with its playing field in the dip.*
3. *Past the remains of the Lloyds signal station and beyond the public house and cafeteria to continue along the undulating cliff top as far as Belle Tout* **(C).**
4. *From Belle Tout the track continues a little inland, descending towards the old coastguard look-out station before dropping down into Birling Gap* **(D).**
5. *The way back begins along a footpath skirting the right hand side of the Beachy Head coast road.*
6. *Immediately below Belle Tout turn left across the road and along a concrete road to Cornish Farm.*

WALK 2 – DOWNLANDS

Access/Parking:	Route 5 or 6 Eastbourne Bus from Gildredge Road opposite Eastbourne railway station to Meads; alight at Carlisle Road, ascend the hill crossing the opening of Gaudick Road and Denton Road, bear right into Paradise Drive, pass the turning into Links Road and the start of the South Downs Way (Bridleway Section) is on the left. Kerbside parking is permitted in Carlisle Road.
Map Reference:	Landranger 199 grid reference 598981
Distance:	8½ miles (14km)
Time to Allow:	4 hours
Terrain:	Steep ascent and descent to start and finish the walk otherwise moderately easy walking across golf course and downland
Toilets/Refreshments:	None
Route:	Eastbourne – Downs Golf Course – Pea Down – Eastdean Down – Crapham Down – Warren Hill – Eastbourne

This is the alternative South Downs Way to Walk One although the original route following the South Downs to Jevington. It begins with a steady if exacting climb up Warren Hill to the Downs Golf Course across the A259, rewarded with glorious views across Eastbourne and Pevensey Bay. The return cuts through Pea Down to the outskirts of East Dean before covering the peaceful Crapham Down back to Warren Hill and the descent back to Eastbourne.

Directions:

1. *A map board here shows the route which rises through grass and bushes to Paradise Wood, past the covered in reservoir on the right to a point where the track divides three ways.*
2. *Keep right here where, further right still and almost hidden in the grass, are the rough flint wall remains of an old windmill* **(A) (B).**
3. *Cross the A259 continuing ahead along a wide track across the golf course for 1 mile (1.6km).*

4. *Turn left over a stile, leaving the main track to continue ahead over Willingdon Hill, and follow the contours of the valley which is Pea Down.*
5. *Turn right over the stile beside the dew pond* **(C)** *then left to another stile which leads onto a track (which may be a little overgrown in summer). Follow this track as it swings round left to a third stile which cross and turn right.*
6. *Follow the narrow track between the backs of houses on the outskirts of East Dean as far as the metalled lane where turn right.*
7. *At the A259 turn left and in 200 yards (185m) right across the fields.*
8. *By the farm buildings the main route continues ahead, although a short detour may be made about 50 yards (47m) before them by turning left past the pond to a well preserved flint shepherd's hut with an attractive chimney. Return to the main route downhill to Crapham Down.*
9. *Turn left along the dry downland valley to the road at Warren Hill.*
10. *Cross the road to the car parking area, taking the public bridleway off left, turning right along the public footpath by the Long Distance Footpath marker post downhill to rejoin the outward route by the remains of the old windmill back to where the walk started.*

POINTS OF INTEREST ON THE WALK

(A) Windmill

A mill was recorded on this site as early as 1724 and a little to the north, in a depression in the chalk, stood a post-mill thought to date back to the sixteenth century.

Certainly a bolting house, a rectangular building with mock Gothic facade, was built here and it is also known that in 1752 Thomas Mortimer erected a horizontal mill on the site of the bolting house, actually incorporating the facade. The flint wall remains seen today are approximately 50 feet (15m) in diameter and within these are the excavated base of the bolting house.

There were many variations of horizontal windmills usually with louvred smock erected on a flint base and containing a driving element similar to a large water-wheel mounted on a vertical shaft. The louvres were arranged to admit wind to one side of this rotor only and the power communicated was then taken by the shaft into the building below driving the millstones in the usual manner.

The mill worked for about 15 years but by the 1780's had become derelict and the whole site was extensively pilfered, although during an excavation in 1966 several contemporary items were still unearthed.

(B) Viewpoint

Extensive views over Eastbourne at this point with Langney Point in the foreground and beyond the wide sweep of Pevensey Bay to Bexhill and Hastings 16 miles (26km) away as the crow flies. Inland the Pevensey Levels are a marked contrast to the undulating downland of our present position and further east.

(C) Dewpond

A dewpond is an artificial clay pond which holds rain water and used by shepherds and farmers to water their stock. They were often built in chalk and limestone areas and the oldest of them date back to the seventeenth century although they were still being made as late as the 1940's. Their builders often worked at night digging the symmetrical hollows before lining them with puddled clay. Good ones retain their water even in the driest of weather for the true art was in the positioning of the pond to collect the maximum amount of rainwater running off the land while allowing for as little evaporation as possible.

Contrary to their name they are not designed to gather dew; they are named after their inventor a Mr Dew.

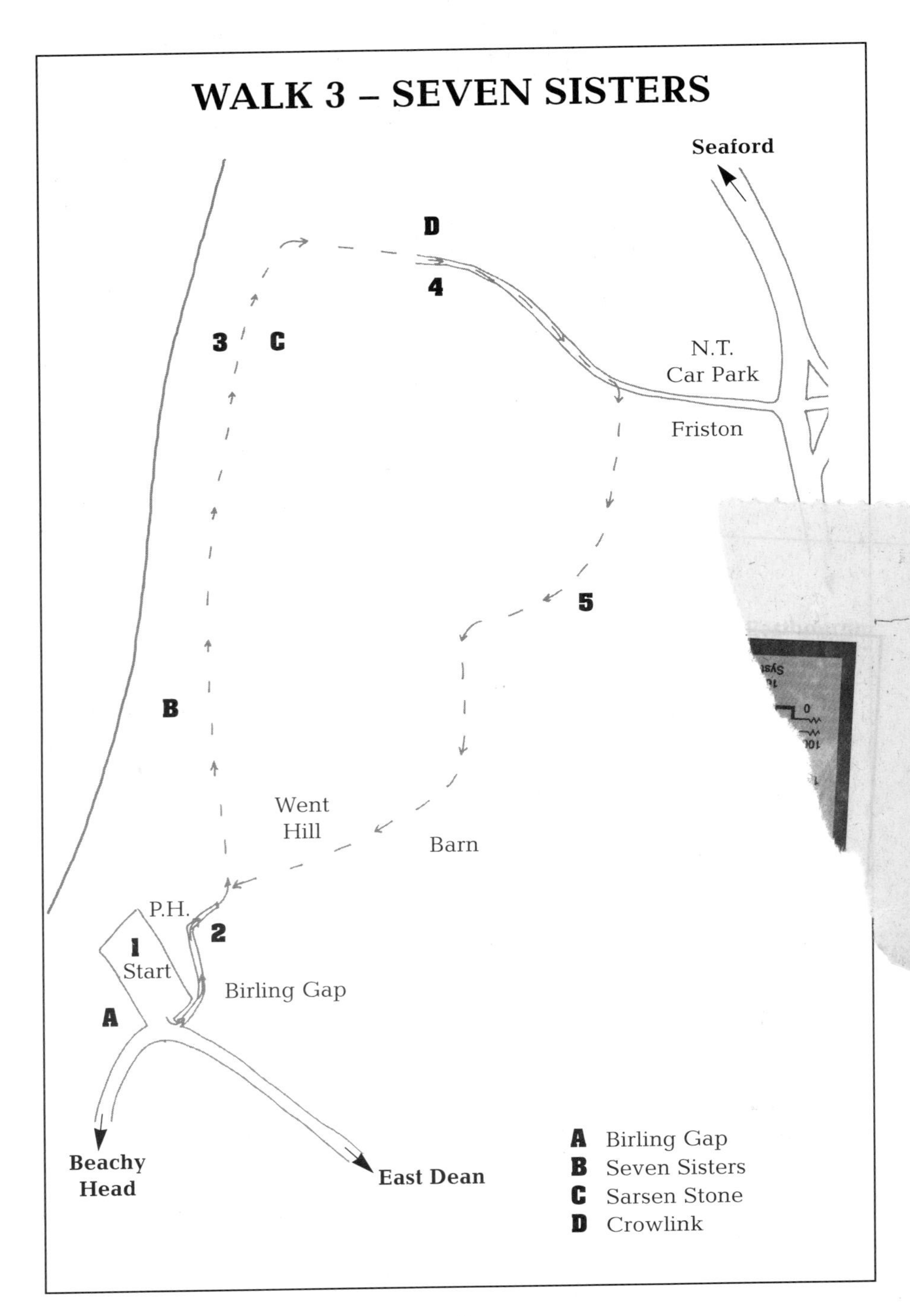
WALK 3 – SEVEN SISTERS
Seaford
D
4
3
C
N.T.
Car Park
Friston
5
B
Went
Hill
Barn
P.H.
2
1
Start
Birling Gap
A
Beachy
Head
East Dean
A Birling Gap
B Seven Sisters
C Sarsen Stone
D Crowlink

The Long Man of Wilmington.

POINTS OF INTEREST ON THE WALK

(A) St Andrew's Church see page 20

(B) The Long Man see page 37

(C) St Peter Folkington

This little church has stood since the mid-thirteenth century, though from the history of this tiny hamlet traced back to pre-Conquest days it is evident that a church of some sort existed on the same site since at least early Norman times. Only 67 feet by 24 feet (20m by 7m), few alterations have been made to this diminutive building of Early English and Perpendicular styles until a general restoration was carried out in 1870 when the vestry was added and the chancel roof rebuilt. Further restorative work was carried out in the early 1960's.

Inside it still retains half a dozen box pews, one on two levels and a monument on the north wall to Viscount Monckton, who as Sir Walter Monckton was adviser to Edward VIII during the Abdication.

(D) Eight Bells Public House see page 22

Folkington

Founded by the Foulk or Folk People who landed at Folkestone in about AD600 this quiet little place is pronounced 'Fowington' although the locals call it 'Fowenton'. It is a charming spot with grace and dignity and a Manor that is secluded and almost lost from view. In the 1960's the village played its part in getting a better deal for badgers drawing the attention of Lady Monkton who, with the aid of her cousin Lord Arran, introduced the Badger Protection Act in the House of Lords.

Nicholas Culpeper, the famous herbalist, lived at Folkington and after being apprenticed to an apothecary set himself up as a student of physic and astrology in the 1640's.

Details of the church of St Peter are on page 63.

NEARBY POINTS OF INTEREST ON THE WALK

Friston Forest

This whole area was once covered with gorse which was cleared and since 1926 over 1600 acres of downland has been converted into a man made forest of mainly beech, Scots and Corsican pine. Goldcrests, linnets and nightingales are frequent visitors to the forest while hoopoes, rare visitors from Africa are sometimes seen in the spring. Marbled whites and dark green fritillaries are some of the butterflies seen in summer and badgers are known to inhabit the undergrowth.

Lullington Heath Nature Reserve

The Reserve was established to conserve the finest chalk heath remaining in Britain. Chalk heath occurs where shallow, acid soils overlie the chalk allowing chalk grassland plants like dropwort and salad burnet to grow alongside heathland species like heather and tormentil.

Until the 1950's these downs were closely grazed by rabbits but after the outbreak of myxomatosis the fine sward became overgrown with gorse and scrub due to lack of grazing. In recent years much of the scrub has been cleared and grazing re-established. Some scrub has been left and is cut regularly to encourage breeding birds like yellow-hammer and white-throat to appear.

The Reserve is situated about 2 miles west of Jevington.

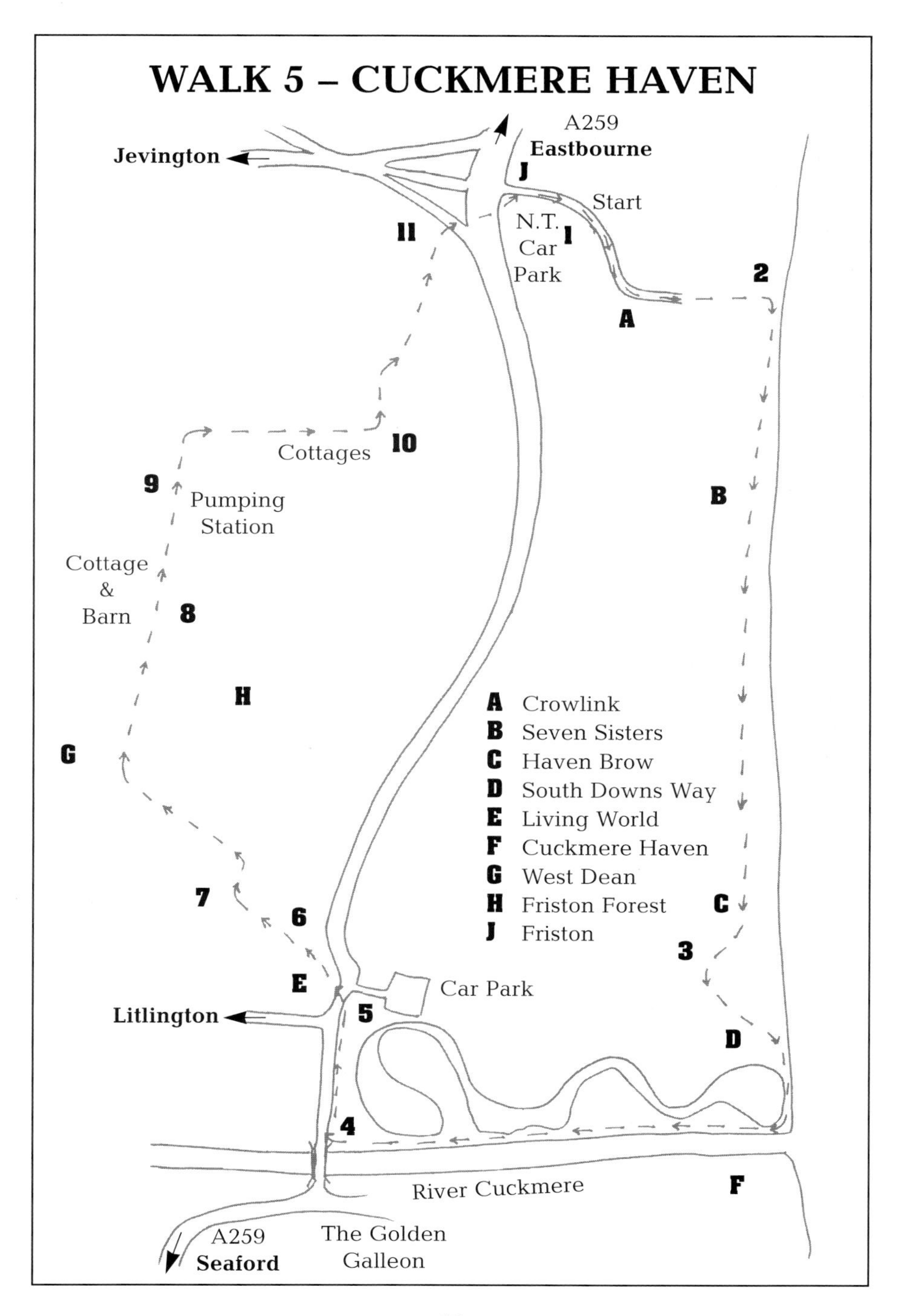
WALK 5 – CUCKMERE HAVEN
A259
Eastbourne
Jevington
J
Start
N.T.
Car
Park
1
11
2
A
10
Cottages
9
Pumping
Station
B
Cottage
&
Barn
8
H
G
A Crowlink
B Seven Sisters
C Haven Brow
D South Downs Way
E Living World
F Cuckmere Haven
G West Dean
H Friston Forest
J Friston
7
6
C
3
E
Car Park
Litlington
5
D
4
River Cuckmere
F
A259
Seaford
The Golden
Galleon

WALK 5 – CUCKMERE HAVEN

Access/Parking:	National Trust car park at Crowlink off the A259 at Friston
Map Reference:	Landranger 199 grid reference 550979
Distance:	7½ miles (12km)
Time to Allow:	4 hours
Terrain:	Over several moderately steep ascents along the Seven Sisters coastline then using well defined tracks through Friston Forest on the return route
Toilets/Refreshments:	At Cuckmere Haven
Route:	Crowlink – Seven Sisters – Cuckmere Haven – West Dean – Friston Forest – Friston – Crowlink

This is a splendid walk with absolutely everything!

From the National Trust car park the walk begins with a delightful stretch into the tiny hamlet of Crowlink affording splendid views across the downland to the English Channel. Then the next section traverses the Seven Sisters as far as Cuckmere Haven where there is an opportunity to pause for refreshment or indulge in the many activities on offer there. From here the route descends into the solitude of West Dean, one of East Sussex treasures, then through the shades of Friston Forest back to the church at Friston and along to Crowlink to conclude the walk.

Directions:

1. *Follow the metalled road down through Crowlink* **(A)** *to the cliff edge.*
2. *Turn right along the cliff path over four of the Seven Sisters* **(B);** *Brass Point, Rough Brow, Short Brow and Haven Brow* **(C).**

3. *Follow a wire fence on the right to a stile halfway down the hill, keeping to a steep chalk path to where a South Downs Way* **(D)** *plinth directs the route across the shingle beach before following the straight river along its east bank to Exceat Bridge.*
4. *Cross the stile to the road, turning right along the footpath alongside the A259 as far as the Living World Exhibition Centre* **(E).**
5. *Cross the road by the car park continuing alongside one of the Centre's buildings where a sign confirms the route.*
6. *Over the stile and straight up the field ahead, crossing the stile in the wall where there are magnificent views back across Cuckmere Haven* **(F).**
7. *Turn right over the wall then left at the acorn marker post to West Dean* **(G)** *descending the long staircase and turning right at the bottom along a Public Bridleway into Friston Forest* **(H).**
8. *Pass the cottage and barn on the left, keeping straight ahead at the cross-tracks.*
9. *Keep to the main track (left) by the pumping station turning right at the T-junction by the wall, continuing past a pair of cottages on the right along a footpath into the woods.*
10. *Turn left at the T-junction at the end of the wall then sharp right back into the woods on reaching a small clearing.*
11. *Climb up and over the steps back to the A259 at Friston church* **(J)** *then along the unmade road back to the car park.*

The Cuckmere Valley and part of Friston Forest.

The Cuckmere Valley looking towards Cuckmere Haven.

POINTS OF INTEREST ON THE WALK

(A) Crowlink see page 31

(B) Seven Sisters see page 60

(C) Haven Brow

From the top of Haven Brow splendid views afford the meandering River Cuckmere as it weaves its way up the Cuckmere Valley to Exceat Bridge and the straight channel that was cut in 1846 to by-pass these meanders to prevent flooding. On the opposite side of the Haven are a neat little row of coastguard cottages with the white cliffs of Seaford Head stretching beyond.

(D) South Downs Way see page 52

(E) Living World Exhibition Centre see page 33

(F) Cuckmere Haven see page 32

(G) West Dean see page 34

(H) Friston Forest see page 64

(J) Friston see page 19

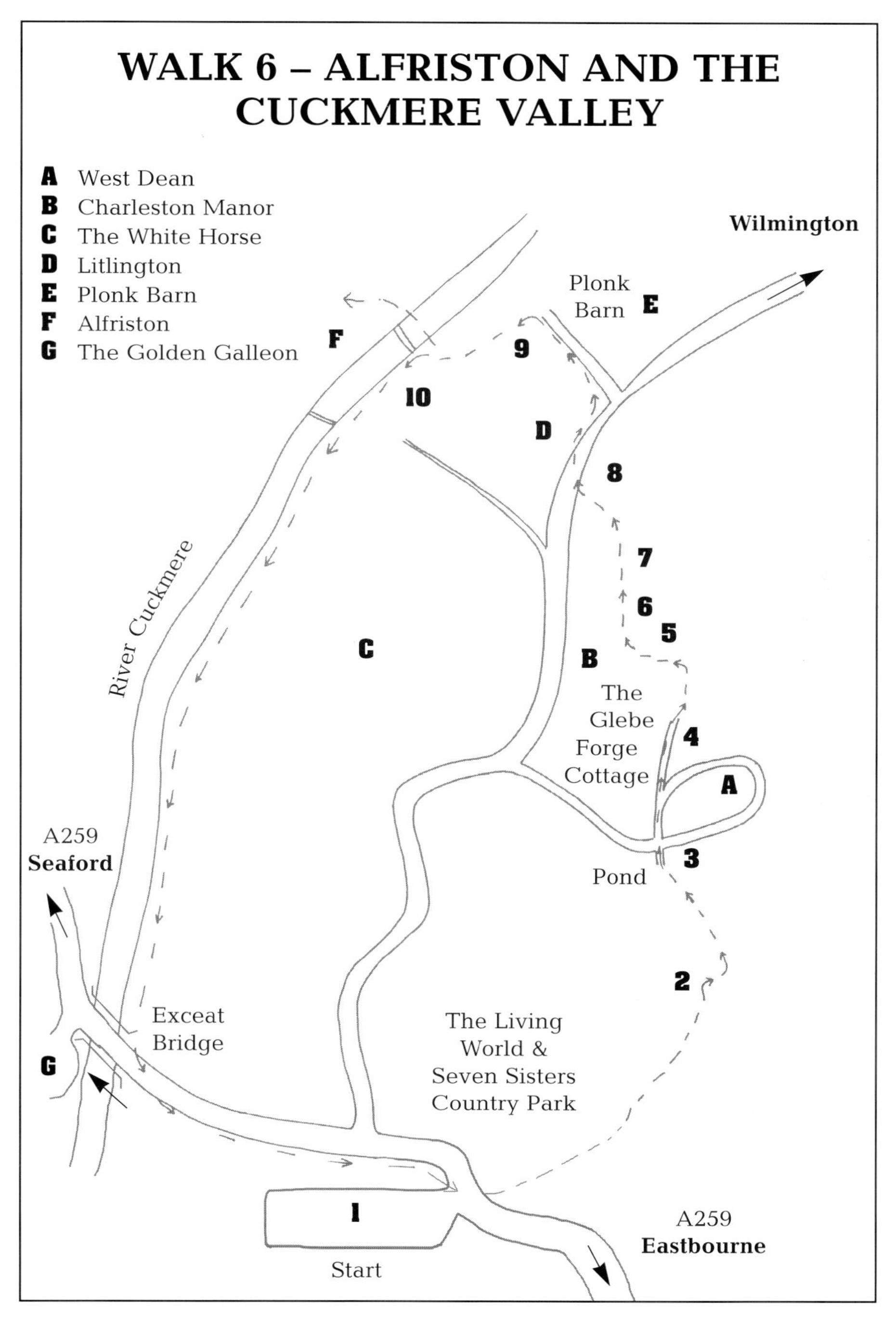
WALK 6 – ALFRISTON AND THE CUCKMERE VALLEY
A West Dean
B Charleston Manor
C The White Horse
D Litlington
E Plonk Barn
F Alfriston
G The Golden Galleon
Wilmington
Plonk Barn
E
F
9
10
D
8
7
6
5
B
C
River Cuckmere
The Glebe Forge Cottage
4
A
3
Pond
A259
Seaford
2
Exceat Bridge
The Living World & Seven Sisters Country Park
G
1
Start
A259
Eastbourne

WALK 6 – ALFRISTON AND THE CUCKMERE VALLEY

Access/Parking:	Car park opposite the Living World Exhibition Centre
Map Reference:	Landranger 199 grid reference 519995
Distance:	7¾ miles (12.8km)
Time to Allow:	4 hours
Terrain:	A steady climb up from the car park followed by a steep staircase down into West Dean. Two more steady ascents before dropping down into Litlington from where the rest of the walk is on level ground
Toilets/Refreshments:	At the Living World, Exceat Bridge; Plough and Harrow public house, Litlington; Litlington Tea Gardens and numerous pubs and restaurants in Alfriston
Route:	Exceat Bridge – West Dean – Litlington – Alfriston – River Cuckmere – Exceat Bridge

Although the start of this walk retraces part of the previous offering it soon takes on its own identity offering an opportunity to take a short detour round the delightful placidity of West Dean before delving further into Friston Forest emerging at the rear of Charleston Manor. A short stretch along the South Downs Way offers good views across the Cuckmere Valley to the White Horse on its elevated position on The High and Over before the route drops into Litlington with its choice of refreshments, pretty cottages and Norman church. The terrain changes dramatically here, keeping on the level to Plonk Barn where a little bridge takes the South Downs Way into Alfriston, the Capital of the Downs. The return from here keeps to the bank of the River Cuckmere all the way back to Exceat Bridge.

Directions:

1. *Cross the road from the Car Park, turning left between the buildings and over the stile signposted South Downs Way.*

2. *Over the wall stile on the crest of the hill before turning right then left down the long staircase into West Dean* **(A)**.
3. *Pass the pond on the left continuing ahead past Forge Cottage (turn right at the road to take the short detour round the village, rejoining the main route at Forge Cottage).*
4. *Keep right at the Glebe, over the stile and turn left at the yellow waymarker signposted Litlington.*
5. *Cross a stile to descend rough steps to the rear of Charleston Manor* **(B)** *of which only the slightest glimpse is possible.*
6. *Pass over the drive and along a narrow path before turning sharp right over a stile, following a rising path along the borders of three fields before crossing two more stiles from where there is an uninhibited view of the White Horse* **(C)** *cut into the side of the Downs.*
7. *Keep alongside the right hedge of the next field then down an obvious path to a kissing gate through which turn left at the metalled road then right into Litlington* **(D)**.
8. *Follow the road through the village to the church where a path suddenly appears taking the route past three houses called "Ham" before entering a field over a stile. The route is obvious from here as far as Plonk Barn* **(E)**.
9. *Turn left over the bridge into Alfriston* **(F)**.
10. *Return over the bridge and turn right along the river bank following the Cuckmere all the way back to Exceat Bridge and the Golden Galleon* **(G)**. *Cross the bridge and then follow the path along the main road back to the car park.*

POINTS OF INTEREST ON THE WALK

(A) West Dean see page 34

(B) Charleston Manor see page 35

(C) The White Horse see page 35

(D) Litlington see page 35

(E) Plonk Barn

It sounds as though it ought to contain wine but it is a brick and flint building of no significance save for the fact that it marks the point where the South Downs Way footpath and bridleway meet to continue as one across the bridge into Alfriston. Today it has been modernised and is now a private residence.

The White Horse.

(F) Alfriston

Much has been written about this downland village which was once a Saxon settlement and now justifiably known as the Capital of the Downs. Its fine village square boasts the traditional spreading chestnut tree and a battered market cross, unique in East Sussex and rivalled only by a better example in Chichester in the entire county. It was probably erected in the fifteenth century for Henry IV granted the right to hold a market on Tuesday of each week in 1405. The original cross was hit by a lorry in 1955 and damaged so badly that only a small portion of the original stone could be used in its replacement.

Houses skirting either side of the main street are not merely picturesque but display all the main characteristic materials of the area; timber frames filled with daub and plaster or covered by weather-boarding or rich, red tiles. Here fourteenth and fifteenth century houses, tearooms, shops and restaurants jostle for position along with four inns of unique character.

The most renowned building is the fifteenth century Star Inn with its fascinating carvings and ferocious red lion outside which was once the figurehead of a seventeenth century Dutch warship. This place has been everything in its time from a resting place for pilgrims on their way to and from Chichester to a haunt for smugglers.

Another building of fourteenth century origin is the thatched Old Clergy House, the first property bought by the National Trust in 1896 for the paltry sum of £10. It stands by the edge of the Tye (an old Saxon name for village green) which is dominated by the church of St Andrews, known because of its size as the Cathedral of the Downs. Built about 1360 it is unlike any of its counterparts being constructed all at one time with no later additions. Its list of rectors and vicars go back to 1272 which would suggest an earlier Saxon church occupied the same site although there is no mention in Domesday Book to verify this.

Alfriston: showing the 15th century Star Inn on the left and looking towards the Market Cross. *(Photograph by Sandy Hernu)*

WALK 7 – LULLINGTON CHURCH

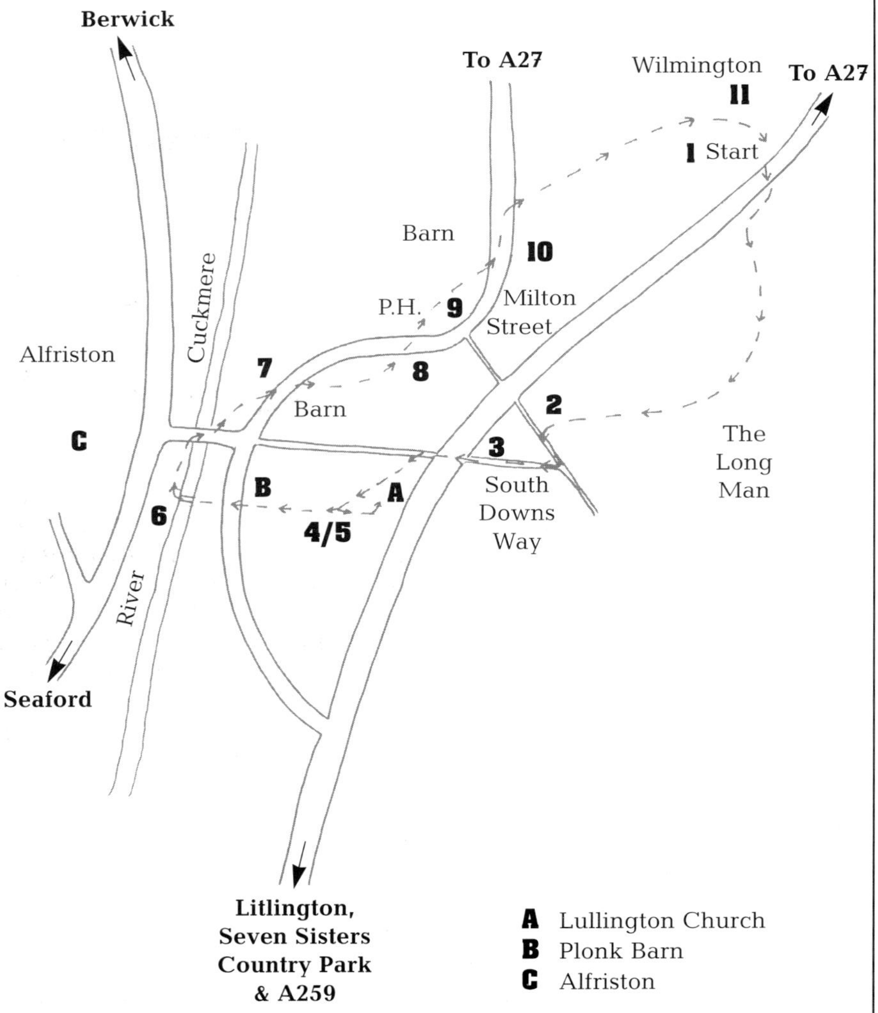

Berwick
To A27
Wilmington
To A27
11
1 Start
Barn
10
P.H.
9
Milton Street
Cuckmere
Alfriston
7
8
Barn
2
C
3
The Long Man
B
A
South Downs Way
6
4/5
River
Seaford
Litlington, Seven Sisters Country Park & A259

A Lullington Church
B Plonk Barn
C Alfriston

WALK 7 – LULLINGTON CHURCH

Access/Parking:	Wilmington Priory/Long Man Car Park
Map Reference:	Landranger 199 grid reference 544042
Distance:	4 miles (6.6km)
Time to Allow:	2 hours
Terrain:	Steady ascent at the Long Man along well trodden path with slight descent into Alfriston. Return along obvious paths across the fields on mainly level ground.
Toilets/Refreshments:	Toilets at the parking place also in Alfriston and Milton Street; Refreshments in Alfriston and at the Sussex Ox, Milton Street.
Route:	Wilmington - Long Man - Lullington Church - Alfriston - Milton Street - Wilmington

A simple walk requiring no great effort yet surprisingly satisfying throughout its duration. It begins from the car park serving Wilmington church and its priory where the views of the Long Man are most memorable and countless pairs of feet have trodden the route to the foot of the chalk figure. From here access is made onto the South Downs Way as it concludes its initial stretch into Alfriston but a detour is soon made from it in order to visit the little church of Lullington standing lonely in a small enclosure. Alfriston is but a short distance away before returning via the hamlet of Milton Street where refreshments may be taken as the route returns to Wilmington affording splendid views of the Long Man across the fields.

Directions:

1. *Take the path from the Car Park to the foot of the Long Man where bear right to the gate.*
2. *Turn left through the gate and continue uphill to the chalk cross-tracks where turn obtusely right onto the South Downs Way.*
3. *Cross straight over at the road turning left over the stile in a few yards to cross the field diagonally right to another stile which cross continuing across the next field.*
4. *At the junction with another path turn left to visit Lullington Church* **(A).**

5. *Return to the path, turning right to retrace steps before carrying on to Plonk Barn* **(B)** *where cross the road to a path which crosses the river into Alfriston* **(C).**
6. *Continue along the river bank to a stile at the next bridge, turning right over the bridge then immediately left over another stile to Arlington, crossing the field diagonally right to the road.*
7. *Turn left at the road then right at a stile opposite the large house (just beyond an open barn on the right) to a second stile in 30 yards (27m) before heading straight across the next field.*
8. *Cross another stile keeping straight ahead over the road to a stile in a high hedge then across a small paddock bearing right of the barn.*
9. *Over yet another stile taking the centre of three options which crosses straight over the next field to a stile leading onto the road.*
10. *The route turns left here but to visit the Sussex Ox turn right and return. In about 70 yards (63m) turn right along a track immediately before the thatched cottage. There are splendid views of the Long Man along this stretch of the walk.*
11. *At the metalled lane turn left then right through a small gate into Wilmington churchyard. Continue to the right past the church and ruined priory back to the car park.*

POINTS OF INTEREST ON THE WALK

(A) Lullington Church

The little church at Lullington stands on a hill yet is almost hidden among a clump of trees. It is one of the smallest churches in Britain but in reality it is just part of the chancel of a much larger church the remains of which can be traced to the West of the entrance. When and how the church was destroyed remains a mystery although tradition has it it was done in Cromwellian times.

The current church is about 16 feet square (4.6m) and seats twenty people. It dates from the thirteenth century and was repaired in 1806 and further restored in 1894.

(B) Plonk Barn see page 71

(C) Alfriston see page 72

WALK 8 – MICHELHAM PRIORY

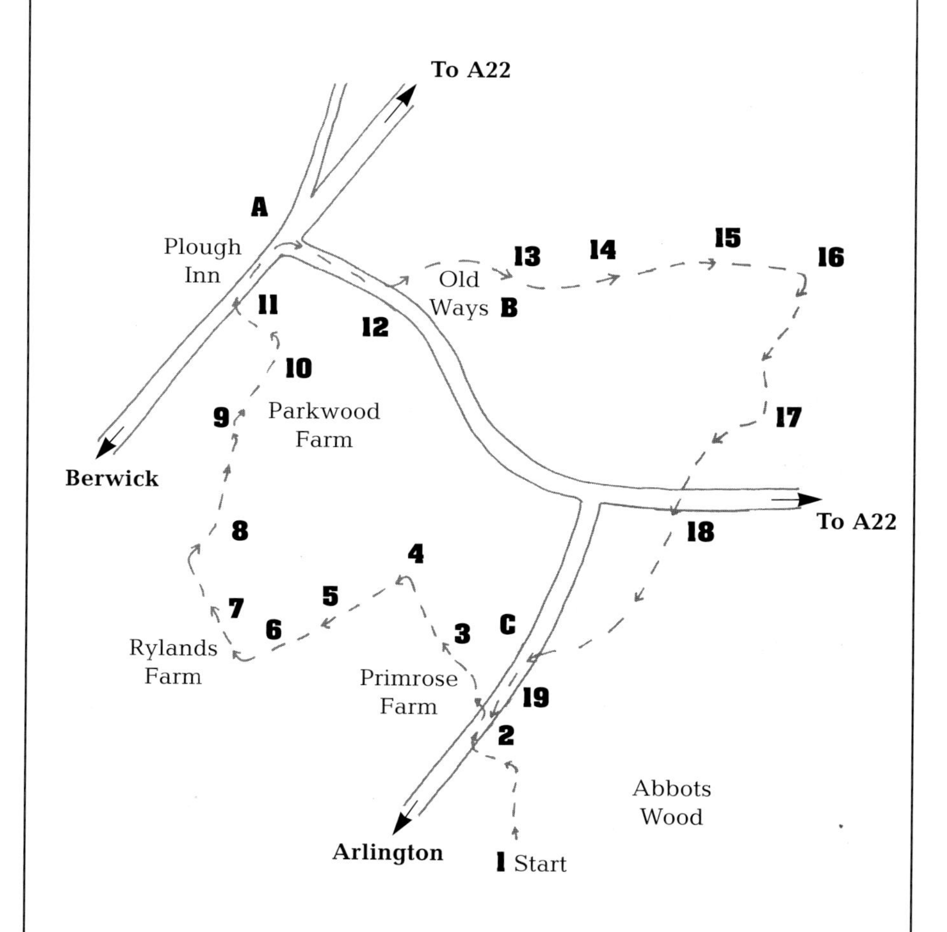

WALK 8 - MICHELHAM PRIORY

Access/Parking:	Car Park in Abbots Wood Nature Reserve
Map Reference:	Landranger 199 grid reference 558073.
Distance:	$6^1/_2$ mile (10.7km)
Time to Allow:	$3^1/_2$ hours
Terrain:	Fairly level ground throughout.
Toilets/Refreshments:	Plough Public House, Dicker. Old Oak Inn, Arlington.
Route:	Abbots Wood – Primrose Farm – The Dicker – Michelham Priory – Abbots Wood.

Dominated by woodland and open countryside this walk visits a village that is gradually being taken over by an institution and gives access to one of the most glorious pieces of England. The outward route begins in the lovely Abbots Wood before crossing farmland to The Dicker, a village that has taken its name from a mansion built at the turn of the last century and is now a school. Michelham Priory, a short detour from the main route, is almost 800 years old although much restored during its long and varied existence. The final stretch of the walk returns to woodland completing an attractive and interesting excursion of Sussex wealdland.

Directions:

1. *From the car park proceed to the right of the toilet block along Forest Walk. As the track swings round right turn off left along a gravel track to the road.*
2. *At the road turn right and in 100 yards (95m) left into Primrose Farm where turn right onto concrete road which follow round left.*
3. *At the end of the concrete road pass through the right hand gate crossing the next field diagonally left along an obvious path to the left of the pylon ahead. Through another gate keeping ahead across a cultivated field.*
4. *Turn left at the telegraph pole at the end of the cultivated field passing a small breeze-block hut, crossing a ditch by a plank bridge before going over a stile by the yellow waymarker.*
5. *Keep ahead across the next field to a stile, keeping to the left of the next field and heading to the right of the pylon ahead.*

6. *At the pylon head diagonally right across the field to a stile in the corner of the field and in 100 yards (95m) over another stile before turning right onto a metalled road.*

7. *Pass the farm buildings on the left, keeping ahead along a gravel track through the trees. Cross the bridge over the River Cuckmere turning right immediately over a stile onto the Wealdway with the river on the right.*

8. *Cross the bridge and in 50 yards (47m) the stile to the left. Head across the next field in the direction of the house to the left of the wood.*

9. *Over two more stiles before bearing left in the direction of the yellow waymarkers along a concrete road then immediately right along the Wealdway, skirting the wood to the right.*

10. *Over the stile onto the golf course, through the double-barred gate and ahead to a stile before turning left alongside a barbed wire fence and over another stile past a pond full of bullrushes on the right to yet another stile leading onto the road.*

11. *Turn right at the road past the Plough Inn turning right at the junction signposted Michelham Priory/Abbots Wood opposite St Bedes School, The Dicker* **(A).**

12. *To visit Michelham Priory* **(B)** *turn left in 1/2 mile (0.8km) and to continue the walk return to the road, turning right and right again in 200 yards (190m) by Oldways, crossing the stile signposted Hailsham and turning right.*

13. *Pass through a wooden gate and along a narrow path between the houses and field (this part may be overgrown in Summer). Over a stile and across a triangular shaped paddock.*

14. *Through a gate by the barns bearing left onto a gravel track over the river. Cross a second bridge, keeping ahead then round right along a rectangular meadow.*

15. *At the stile by the gate keep ahead as the Wealdway turns off left. Cross a plank bridge then over the stile by the yellow waymarker post following a well defined path through the woods.*

16. *Pass through a metal gate before turning right round the boundary of the next field as far as the stile to the right of another metal gate. Turn right along a dirt track which gradually widens before turning off left. Follow this track with glimpses of Arlington Circuit through the trees on the left, keeping to the left hand fence and ignoring all other paths off right.*

17. *At the clearing turn right following a line beneath the overhead power lines. At the deep grooved clay track about 50 yards (48m) before the next pylon turn left, following the track to the road.*

18. *Cross the road and keep ahead to the power lines. Once passing underneath them turn right onto a broad track which penetrates into the woods along an obvious track. Cross the bridge keeping ahead ignoring all other tracks until reaching the road. Turn left at the road along the grass verge, passing Primrose Farm to the Old Oak Inn* **(C).**

19. *Return to the track back into Abbots Wood turning right at the cross-tracks to retrace steps back to the car park.*

POINTS OF INTEREST ON THE WALK

(A) The Dicker see page 44

(B) Michelham Priory see page 45

(C) Old Oak Inn

Built in 1733 as the village poorhouse it did not become an inn until 1834 when it opened on Sundays only for on other days of the week the workers it was intended to serve were too busy working in the woods to avail themselves of its services. Today the inn has a full on licence and offers a varied bill of fare for its customers.